Key Issues Regarding Digital Libraries

Evaluation and Integration

Synthesis Lectures on Information Concepts, Retrieval, and Services

Editor
Gary Marchionini, *University of North Carolina at Chapel Hill*

The series will publish on topics pertaining to information science and applications of technology to information discovery, production, distribution, and management. Potential topics include data models, indexing theory and algorithms, classification, information architecture, information economics, privacy and identity, scholarly communication, bibliometrics and webometrics, personal information management, human information behavior, digital libraries, archives and preservation, cultural informatics, information retrieval evaluation, data fusion, relevance feedback, recommendation systems, question answering, natural language processing for retrieval, text summarization, multimedia retrieval, multilingual retrieval, and exploratory search.

Information Architecture: The Design and Integration of Information Spaces
Wei Ding and Xia Lin
2009

Reading and Writing the Electronic Book
Catherine C. Marshall
2009

Hypermedia Genes: An Evolutionary Perspective on Concepts, Models, and Architectures
Nuno M. Guimarães and Luís M. Carrico
2009

Understanding User-Web Interactions via Web Analytics
Bernard J. (Jim) Jansen
2009

XML Retrieval
Mounia Lalmas
2009

Faceted Search
Daniel Tunkelang
2009

Introduction to Webometrics: Quantitative Web Research for the Social Sciences
Michael Thelwall
2009

Exploratory Search: Beyond the Query-Response Paradigm
Ryen W. White and Resa A. Roth
2009

New Concepts in Digital Reference
R. David Lankes
2009

Automated Metadata in Multimedia Information Systems: Creation, Refinement, Use in
Surrogates, and Evaluation
Michael G. Christel
2009

Key Issues Regarding Digital Libraries: Evaluation and Integration

Rao Shen, Marcos André Gonçalves, and Edward A. Fox

ISBN: 978-3-031-01155-9   paperback
ISBN: 978-3-031-02283-8   ebook

DOI 10.1007/978-3-031-02283-8

A Publication in the Springer series
SYNTHESIS LECTURES ON INFORMATION CONCEPTS, RETRIEVAL, AND SERVICES

Lecture #26
Series Editor: Gary Marchionini, *University of North Carolina at Chapel Hill*
Series ISSN
Synthesis Lectures on Information Concepts, Retrieval, and Services
Print 1947-945X   Electronic 1947-9468

Key Issues Regarding Digital Libraries

Evaluation and Integration

Rao Shen
Yahoo!, USA

Marcos André Gonçalves
Universidade Federal de Minas Gerais, Brazil

Edward A. Fox
Virginia Tech

SYNTHESIS LECTURES ON INFORMATION CONCEPTS, RETRIEVAL, AND SERVICES #26

ABSTRACT

This is the second book based on the 5S (Societies, Scenarios, Spaces, Structures, Streams) approach to digital libraries (DLs). Leveraging the first volume, on Theoretical Foundations, we focus on the key issues of evaluation and integration. These cross-cutting issues serve as a bridge for those interested in DLs, connecting the introduction and formal discussion in the first book, with the coverage of key technologies in the third book, and of illustrative applications in the fourth book. These two topics have central importance in the DL field, allowing it to be treated scientifically as well as practically. In the scholarly world, we only really understand something if we know how to measure and evaluate it. In the Internet era of distributed information systems, we only can be practical at scale if we integrate across both systems and their associated content.

Evaluation of DLs must take place at multiple levels, so we can address the different entities and their associated measures. Thus, for digital objects, we assess accessibility, pertinence, preservability, relevance, significance, similarity, and timeliness. Other measures are specific to higher-level constructs like metadata, collections, catalogs, repositories, and services. We tie these together through a case study of the 5SQual tool, which we designed and implemented to perform an automatic quantitative evaluation of DLs. Thus, across the Information Life Cycle, we describe metrics and software useful to assess the quality of DLs, and demonstrate utility with regard to representative application areas: archaeology and education.

Though integration has been a challenge since the earliest work on DLs, we provide the first comprehensive 5S-based formal description of the DL integration problem, cast in the context of related work. Since archaeology is a fundamentally distributed enterprise, we describe ETANA-DL, for integrating Near Eastern Archeology sites and information. Thus, we show how 5S-based modeling can lead to integrated services and content.

While the first book adopts a minimalist and formal approach to DLs, and provides a systematic and functional method to design and implement DL exploring services, here we broaden to practical DLs with richer metamodels, demonstrating the power of 5S for integration and evaluation.

KEYWORDS

5S framework, 5SQual, archaeology, content, digital libraries (DLs), digital objects, education, evaluation, exploration, formalization, integration, measures, metadata, modeling, services

This book is dedicated to our families,
with thanks for their encouragement, patience, and support.

Contents

List of Tables

List of Figures

Preface

Because of the importance of digital libraries (DLs), we integrated, organized, and condensed our related findings and publications into a single volume version of this book series, ultimately over 600 pages in length, that was successfully used in a semester long class in 2011, as well as field tested at different universities. To make it easier for others to address their need for a DL textbook, we have re-organized the original book into four parts, to cover: introduction and theoretical foundations, key issues, technologies/extensions, and applications. We are confident that this book, and the others in the series, address DL related needs in many computer science, information science, and library science (e.g., LIS) courses, as well as the requirements of researchers, developers, and practitioners.

The main reason is that our 5S (Societies, Scenarios, Spaces, Structures, Streams) framework has broad descriptive power. This is proved in part by the recent expansion of interest related to each of the five Ss, e.g., Social networks, Scenario-based design, geoSpatial databases, Structure-based approaches (e.g., databases, metadata, ontologies, XML), and data Stream management systems.

Book 1, the essential opening to the four book series, has three main parts. Chapter 1 is the key to 5S, providing a theoretical foundation for the field of DLs in a gentle, intuitive, and easy-to-apply manner. Chapter 2 explains how 5S can be applied to DLs, in two ways. First, it covers the most important services of DLs: browsing, searching, discovery, and visualization. Second, it demonstrates how 5S helps with the design, implementation, and evaluation of an integrated DL (ETANA-DL, for archaeology). The third part of this book, made up by five appendices, demonstrates how 5S enables a formal treatment of DLs. It is freely accessible, online, at https://sites.google.com/a/morganclaypool.com/dlibrary/.

Appendix A gives a small set of definitions that cover the mathematical preliminaries underlying our work. Appendix B builds on that set to define each of the five Ss, and then uses them to define what we consider a minimal DL. Thus, we allow people asking "Is X a digital library?" to answer that question definitively. Appendix C moves from a minimalist perspective to show how 5S can be used in a real, interesting, and complex application domain: archaeology. Appendix D builds upon all the definitions in Appendices A-C, to describe some key results of using 5S. This includes lemmas, proofs, and 5SSuite (software based on 5S). Finally, Appendix E, the Glossary, explains key terminology. Concluding the work is an extensive Bibliography, and a helpful Index.

This current book, Book 2 two in the series, discusses key issues in the DL field: evaluation and integration. It covers the Information Life Cycle, metrics, and software to help evaluate DLs. It uses both archaeology and electronic theses and dissertations, to provide additional context, since addressing quality in highly distributed DLs is particularly challenging.

In the following two books of this series are further elaborations of the 5S framework, as well as a comprehensive overview of related work on DLs.

Book 3 describes six case studies, of extensions beyond a minimal DL. Its chapters cover: complex objects, subdocuments, ontologies, classification, text extraction, and security. *Regarding complex objects:* While many DLs focus on digital objects and/or metadata objects, with support for complex objects, they could easily be extended to handle aggregation and packaging. Fingerprint matching provides a useful context, since there are complex inter-relationships among crime scenes, latent fingerprints, individuals, hands, fingers, fingerprints, and images. *Regarding subdocuments:* This builds upon work on superimposed information, closely related to hypertext, hypermedia, and annotation. Case studies cover fish images and Flickr. *Regarding ontologies:* We address this key area of knowledge management, also integral to the Semantic Web. As a context, we consider our Crisis, Tragedy, and Recovery Network (CTRnet). That is quite broad, and involves interesting ontology development problems. *Regarding classification:* We cover this core area of information retrieval and machine learning, as well as Library and Information Science (LIS). The context is electronic theses and dissertations (ETDs), since many of these works have no categories that can be found in their catalog or metadata records, and since none are categorized at the level of chapters. *Regarding text extraction:* Our coverage also is in the context of ETDs, where the high-level structure should be identified, and where the valuable and voluminous sets of references can be isolated and shifted to canonical representations. *Regarding security:* While many DLs support open access, it has been clear since the early 1990s that industrial acceptance of DL systems and technologies depends on their being trusted, requiring an integrated approach to security.

Book 4 completes the series, focusing on DL applications, from a 5S perspective. Its chapters cover how to handle: images, education, social networks, e-science (including bioinformatics and simulations), and geospatial information. *Regarding images:* We move into the multimedia field, focusing on Content-based Image Retrieval (CBIR)—making use, for context, of the previously discussed work on fish images and CTRnet. *Regarding education:* We describe systems for collecting, sharing, and providing access to educational resources, namely the AlgoViz and Ensemble systems. This is important since there has been considerable investment in DLs to help in education, all based on the fact that devising high-quality educational resources is expensive, making sharing and reuse highly beneficial. *Regarding social networks:* We address very popular current issues, on the societies side, namely social networks and personalization. *Regarding e-science:* There has only been a limited adaptation and extension of DLs to this important domain. Simulation aids many disciplines to test models and predictions on computers, addressing questions not feasible through other approaches to experimentation. More broadly, in keeping with progress toward e-science, where data sets and shared information supports much broader theories and investigations, we cover (using the SimDL and CINET projects as context) storing and archiving, as well as access and visualization, dealing not only with metadata, but also with specifications of experiments, experimental results, and derivative versions: summaries, findings, reports, and publications. *Regarding geospatial information:* Many GIS-related technologies are now readily available in cell phones, cameras, and GPS systems. Our coverage (that uses the CTRnet project as context) connects that with metadata, images, and maps.

How can computer scientists connect with all this? Though some of the early curricular guidelines advocated coverage of information, and current guidelines refer to the area of information management, generally courses in this area have focused instead either on data or knowledge. Fortunately, Virginia Tech has had graduate courses on information retrieval since the early 1970s and a senior course on 'Multimedia, Hypertext, and Information Access' since the early 1990s. Now, there are offerings at many universities on multimedia, or with titles including keywords like 'Web' or 'search'. Perhaps parts of this book series will provide a way for computing programs to address all areas of information management, building on a firm, formal, integrated approach. Further, computing professionals should feel comfortable with particular Ss, especially Structures (as in data structures) and Spaces (as in vector spaces), and to lesser extents Streams (related to multimedia) and Scenarios (related to human-computer interaction). Today, especially, there is growing interest in Societies (as in social networks).

How can information scientists connect with all this? Clearly, they are at home with 'information' as a key construct. Streams (e.g., sequences of characters, or bitstreams) provide a first basis for all types of information. Coupled with Structures, they lead to all types of structured streams, as in documents and multimedia. Spaces may be less clear, but GIS systems are becoming ubiquitous, connecting with GPS, cell phone, Twitter, and other technologies. Scenarios, especially in the form of Services, are at the heart of most information systems. Societies, including users, groups, organizations, and a wide variety of social networks, are central, especially with human-centered design. Thus, information science can easily connect with 5S, and DLs are among the most important types of information systems. Accordingly, this book series may fit nicely into capstone courses in information science or information systems. Further, our handling of 'information' goes well beyond the narrow view associated with electrical engineering or even computer science; we connect content representations with context and application, across a range of human endeavors, and with semantics, pragmatics, and knowledge.

How can library scientists connect with all this? One might argue that many of the librarians of the future must be trained as digital librarians. Thus, this work should fit nicely into library science programs. While it could fit into theory or capstone courses, it also might serve well in introductory courses, if the more formal parts are skipped. Alternatively, Book 1 might work well early in a library school program, Book 2 could fit midway in the program, and the last two books might be covered in specialized courses that connect with technologies or applications. Further, those studying archival science might find the entire series to be of interest, though some topics like preservation are not covered in detail.

How can researchers connect with all this? We hope that those interested in formal approaches will help us expand the coverage of concepts reported herein. A wonderful goal would be to have an elegant formal basis, and useful framework, for all types of information systems. We also hope that the theses and dissertations related to this volume, all online (thanks to Virginia Tech's ETD initiative), will provide an even more in-depth coverage of the key topics covered herein. We hope you can build on this foundation to aid in your own research, as you advance the field further.

How can developers connect with all this? We hope that the concepts, ideas, methods, techniques, systems, and approaches described will guide you to develop, implement, and deploy even better DLs. There should be less time spent "reinventing the wheel." Perhaps this will stimulate the emergence of a vibrant software and services industry as more and more DLs emerge. Further, if there is agreement on key concepts, then there should be improvements in: interoperability, integration, and understanding. Accordingly, we hope you can leverage this work to advance practices as well as provide better systems and services.

Even if you, the reader, do not fit clearly into the groups discussed above, we hope you nevertheless will find this book series interesting. Given the rich content, we trust that those interested in DLs, or in related systems, will find this book to be intellectually satisfying, illuminating, and helpful. We hope the full series will help move DLs forward into a science as well as a practice. We hope too that our four book series will broadly address the needs of the next generation of digital librarians. Please share with us and others what ways you found this work to be useful and helpful!

Rao Shen, Marcos André Gonçalves, and Edward A. Fox
February 2013

Acknowledgments

Since this book is the second in a series of four books, and draws some definitions and other elements from content that either was presented in the first book, or will appear in the following three books, it is important to acknowledge the contributions of all of the other co-authors from the full series: Monika Akbar, Pranav Angara, Yinlin Chen, Lois M. Delcambre, Noha Elsherbiny, Eric Fouh, Nádia P. Kozievitch, Spencer Lee, Jonathan Leidig, Lin Tzy Li, Mohamed Magdy Gharib Farag, Uma Murthy, Sung Hee Park, Venkat Srinivasan, Ricardo da Silva Torres, and Seungwon Yang.

Likewise, we thank our many students, friends, collaborators, co-authors, and colleagues. In particular, we thank students who have collaborated in these matters, including: Pavel Calado, Yuxin Chen, Kiran Chitturi, Fernando Das Neves, Shahrooz Feizabadi, Robert France, Nithiwat Kampanya, Rohit Kelapure, S.H. Kim, Neill Kipp, Aaron Krowne, Sunshin Lee, Bing Liu, Ming Luo, Paul Mather, Unni. Ravindranathan, W. Ryan Richardson, Ohm Sornil, Hussein Suleman, Wensi Xi, Baoping Zhang, and Qinwei Zhu.

Further, we thank faculty and staff, at a variety of universities and other institutions, who have collaborated, including: Paul Bogen II, Lillian Cassel, Vinod Chachra, Hsinchun Chen, Debra Dudley, Roger Ehrich, Joanne Eustis, Weiguo Fan, James Flanagan, James French, Richard Furuta, Dan Garcia, C. Lee Giles, Martin Halbert, Eberhard Hilf, Gregory Hislop, John Impagliazzo, Filip Jagodzinski, Douglas Knight, Deborah Knox, Alberto Laender, Carl Lagoze, Susan Marion, Gail McMillan, Claudia Medeiros, Manuel Perez Quinones, Naren Ramakrishnan, Frank Shipman, and Layne Watson.

Clearly, however, with regard to this volume, special thanks go to the co-authors. Each has played a key role in the unfolding of the theory, practice, systems, and usability of what is described herein. Regarding 5S, Marcos André Gonçalves helped launch our formal framework[1]. Rao Shen has worked hard to finalize this book[2].

In addition, we acknowledge the support of the many sponsors of the research described in this volume. Our fingerprint work was supported by Award No. 2009-DN-BX-K229 from the National Institute of Justice, Office of Justice Programs, U.S. Department of Justice. The opinions, findings, and conclusions or recommendations expressed in this publication are those of the authors and do not necessarily reflect those of the Department of Justice.

Some of the material is based upon work supported by the National Science Foundation (NSF) under Grant Nos. CCF-0722259, DUE-9752190, DUE-9752408, DUE-0121679, DUE-0121741,

---

[1]Various sections of this work are based on the Virginia Tech dissertation of Marcos Gonçalves [35], "Streams, Structures, Spaces, Scenarios, and Societies (5S): A Formal Digital Library Framework and Its Applications," © 2004. Used with permission.
[2]Various figures and sections of this work are based on the Virginia Tech dissertation of Rao Shen [103], "Applying the 5S Framework to Integrating Digital Libraries," © 2006. Used with permission.

DUE-0136690, DUE-0333531, DUE-0333601, DUE-0435059, DUE-0532825, DUE-0840719, IIS-9905026, IIS-9986089, IIS-0002935, IIS-0080748, IIS-0086227, IIS-0090153, IIS-0122201, IIS-0307867, IIS-0325579, IIS-0535057, IIS-0736055, IIS-0910183, IIS-0916733, ITR-0325579, OCI-0904844, OCI-1032677, and SES-0729441. Any opinions, findings, and conclusions or recommendations expressed in this material are those of the authors and do not necessarily reflect the views of the National Science Foundation.

This work has been partially supported by NIH MIDAS project 2U01GM070694-7, DTRA CNIMS Grant HDTRA1-07-C-0113, and R&D Grant HDTRA1-0901-0017.

We thank corporate and institutional sponsors, including Adobe, AOL, CNI, Google, IBM, Microsoft, NASA, NCR, OCLC, SOLINET, SUN, SURA, UNESCO, US Dept. Ed. (FIPSE), and VTLS. A variety of institutions have supported tutorials or courses, including AUGM, CETREDE, CLEI, IFLA-LAC, and UFC.

Visitors and collaborators from Brazil, including from FUA, UFMG, and UNICAMP, have been supported by CAPES (4479-09-2), FAPESP, and CNPq. Our collaboration in Mexico had support from CONACyT, while that in Germany was supported by DFG. Students in our VT-MENA program in Egypt have been supported through that program.

Rao Shen, Marcos André Gonçalves, and Edward A. Fox
February 2013

CHAPTER 1

Evaluation

Abstract: Evaluation is a necessity if scientific studies of digital libraries are to proceed and have impact. We draw from the 5S formal framework to derive a list of quality dimensions and indicators. We designed, implemented, and evaluated 5SQual, a tool intended for automatic quantitative evaluation of some of the most important components of a digital library (DL).

1.1 INTRODUCTION

Because of the importance of digital libraries and their broad applicability, greater attention has been given to their evaluation, especially regarding the utility, usability, and cost of these systems. Identifying what makes a DL a system of good quality, with the potential to satisfy its users, can be difficult and hard to summarize, since it depends on which aspects are considered. As has been pointed out by Fuhr et al. [31], when evaluating quality, people interested in DLs have disparate views of these systems and, as a consequence, focus on different aspects that are relevant to their specific point of view.

1.2 RELATED WORK

One of the fields that has been impacted by evaluation methods and methodologies is Information Retrieval. This field deals with a basic human need: information. Donna Harman [45] explains where different information retrieval evaluation methodologies came from and how they have continued to adapt to the vastly changed environment in the search engine world today. It covers recent batch evaluations, examining the methodologies used in the various open evaluation campaigns such as TREC, NTCIR (emphasizing Asian languages), CLEF (emphasizing European languages), INEX (emphasizing semi-structured data), etc. It includes how the test collection techniques were modified and how the metrics were changed to better reflect operational environments. For example, commercial search engine companies employ recently proposed metrics such nDCG (based on graded relevance judgments [52]) to evaluate the performance of their information retrieval systems.

Another evaluation method used with commercial search engines is called bucket testing. Whenever a new ranking algorithm needs to be tested, a small set of users is randomly assigned to a traffic bucket (called testing bucket) and the new ranking algorithm is used to generate the search results for this set of users. The metric scores for this bucket then are contrasted with scores for a control bucket which uses the production ranker. Comparisons are drawn over the same period of time to avoid interference from temporal changes in user behavior (for example from holidays, weekends, or breaking-news events). For every bucket, there may be a study of metrics such as clickthrough rate (CTR), search volume (search page views), search intensity (searches per user), and revenue per search (RPS).

As expected, evaluation is also a very vital research interest in the DL domain. This has led to a growth of the literature in the main conferences and journals. Marchionini et al. [69] argue that DL evaluation must be rooted in information needs, characteristics, and contexts of potential users, because DLs are built to serve communities of people. As well as the various evaluation methods used for information retrieval, different approaches to evaluate the success of a DL have been studied (e.g., [31], [32], [59], [68], [98], [99], [100], [103], and [116]), involving users, collections, and systems, aimed at identifying generalizable metrics and context specific methods. The difference here is that not only the effectiveness of a given service needs to be evaluated (e.g., in terms of the quality of a ranking produced by searches), but also many other aspects need to be considered regarding content, services, and ultimately user satisfaction.

Another reason for multiple DL evaluation proposals is that different communities have different perceptions regarding the nature of digital libraries. Thus, while the computer science community may focus on technical aspects of evaluation, the library and information science community may emphasize social-economic issues. Further, different approaches to evaluation are engendered by the several underlying models explaining DL concepts, e.g., the 5S framework and the DELOS Reference Model [12].

To provide a general perspective of the digital library evaluation domain, a DL evaluation ontology named DiLEO was devised to reveal explicitly the key concepts and their relationships [117]. It combines and integrates several scientific paradigms, approaches, methods, techniques, and tools. DiLEO has two main layers. The strategic layer covers the main concepts that define the purpose and the scope of an evaluation and relate it to other studies. The procedural layer is composed of classes that model the practice of evaluation initiatives. These classes describe an evaluation activity in terms of processes, constraints, and requirements. DiLEO can be a useful tool to explore the digital library evaluation domain, draw specific conclusions, and make informed decisions. Added value features of DiLEO support comparative studies between different evaluation initiatives, and assist with effective digital library evaluation planning.

Since data quality is a major concern in digital libraries, it is important to be able to measure the (loss of) quality of metadata that is automatically generated by semantic techniques. One approach is through user studies. Thus, in [114] is reported an analysis of the loss of quality due to the use of statistical techniques for automatic metadata creation (namely taxonomies of author keywords and tag clouds). Three measures were considered: degree of category coverage (DCC), semantic word bandwidth (SWB), and relevance of covered terms (RCT).

A primary source of data regarding the operation and use of DLs is logs. Works such as [40] and [57] present standards for DL log formats, with the goal of recording data for the evaluation of DLs. In [40], an XML log format is described that captures detailed information about system behavior and access to its services, storing data that indicate critical details about user interactions with the DL, thus providing valuable information for system evaluation. [57] builds on that work and proposes a multilevel record scheme for DL logging. Such formats are very important for tools such as 5SQual [61], which have evolved from work on DL models (e.g., 5S).

1.2.1   DL MODELS AND EVALUATION

Theories have evolved in parallel regarding: DLs (e.g., the 5S framework), Information System (IS) success and adoption, and information-seeking behavior. They provide foundations that can be integrated to help answer the question: What is a successful DL? At the same time, prior research suggests the need for a more comprehensive view of DL success. More broadly, there have been calls for research to empirically validate and extend IS success and adoptions models into varying contexts. Motivated by these calls for research and the increasing number of DL users with varying skills and from different backgrounds and cultures, we seek to answer the question: What is the appropriate model of DL success, from the perspective of end users (DL patrons)? Then, the success of DL from an end-user perspective is defined in a DL success model [105].

One approach is in connection with work on the DELOS Reference Model [12]. In particular, [50] discussed the premises underlying a novel Policy and Quality Interoperability Framework in the context of that model. This takes into account the preliminary outcomes and the recommendations of the Policy and Quality Working Groups of the EU co-funded project *Digital Library Interoperability, Best Practices, and Modeling Foundations (DL.org)*.

There are other DL evaluation models developed recently. An alternative, holistic, model for DL evaluation was prepared by applying a three-stage research approach: exploration, confirmation, and verification [123]. During the exploration stage, a literature review was conducted, and then an interview along with card sorting was employed to collect perceptions from DL experts with emphasis on determining what criteria should be used in DL evaluation. Then, the identified criteria were used for developing an online survey during the confirmation stage. Different DL stakeholders, with different backgrounds, were asked to rate the importance of each criterion to DL evaluation. Survey respondents (431 in total) from 22 countries rated the criteria. The holistic model was constructed by utilizing descriptive and inferential statistical techniques. Its holistic nature was ensured through: (1) incorporation of various DL stakeholders perspectives in light of Marchionini's [69] multifaceted evaluation approach, and (2) inclusion of all digital library levels suggested by Saracevic's stratified information retrieval model [99]. Eventually, in the verification stage, selected criteria from the model were tested in the context of searching and evaluating an operational DL.

A multidimensional and hierarchical model for quality evaluation of digital libraries (LibEval) was proposed and tested [8]. A convenience sample of 252 undergraduate and graduate students was used. Data was collected in October 2010 by means of a paper-and-pencil questionnaire. Results from a confirmatory factor analysis utilizing structural equation modelling techniques confirmed the existence of a second-order factor construct (Quality of Digital Library) and five first-order dimensions, namely: interface quality, system quality, information quality, service quality, and contextual factors. The results from this study show empirically that the five dimensions are distinct manifestations of the quality of DLs. The user perceives and evaluates the quality of a digital library globally and in each dimension. The LibEval instrument can be utilized to assess the quality of DLs from the general user's perspective.

An organizational model for evaluating and managing DLs was proposed in [56]. The approach is based on Porter's value chain model of organizations, and evaluation logic models, and focuses on evaluating DLs as sociotechnical phenomena that serve diverse communities, domains, and audiences.

Given all of these models, it is appropriate to work to combine the various factors and approaches already studied into a comprehensive approach. Accordingly, we seek below to provide a formal foundation, building upon the 5S framework, and to apply it to real systems by collecting and analyzing appropriate data, thus addressing the observation that evaluation theorists and practitioners do not communicate well [99]. 5SQual [61] addresses these challenges; it is a tool that implements and follows a theoretical quality model for DLs, and that can help administrators in the evaluation of real DLs.

1.3 FORMALIZATION

We draw from the 5S formal framework, as well as from our own experience in building DLs since 1991, to derive the list of quality dimensions described below. We follow the standard terminology used in the social sciences [6]. We use the term *composite quality indicator*[1] (or in short *quality indicator*) to refer to the proposed quantities, instead of the stronger term *quality measure*. Only after one has a number of indicators, and they are validated[2] and tested for reliability,[3] can they be composed into reliable "measures." Despite partial tests of validity (for example, through focus groups[4]) the proposed quality indicators do not qualify as measures yet. Also, it should be stressed that the proposed quantities are only approximations of or give quantified indication of a quality dimension. They should not be interpreted as a complete specification of a quality dimension, since more factors/variables could be relevant than are specified here. We will, however, reserve the right to use the term "measure" when talking about standard measures that have long been used by the CS/LIS communities. The distinction should be clear in context.

Table 1.1 shows a summary of proposed candidate dimensions of quality for some of the most important DL concepts defined above and factors affecting the measurement of the corresponding quality dimensions.[5] The following sections explain these indicators in detail by:

1. motivating them and discussing their meaning/utilization;

---

[1]An indicator composed of two or more simpler indicators or variables.

[2]According to [6], validity refers to the extent to which a specific measurement provides data that relate to commonly accepted meanings of a particular concept. There are numerous yardsticks for determining validity: face validity, criterion validity, content validity, and construct validity.

[3]Also according to [6], reliability refers to the likelihood that a given measurement procedure will yield the same description of a given phenomena if that measurement is repeated.

[4]A type of face validity.

[5]For simplicity, we focus on a DL concept and an indicator, not mentioning all other DL concepts that also relate. Thus, while we assign "relevance" to "digital object," we are aware that users and queries clearly are involved too.

2. formally defining them and specifying their corresponding numerical computation; and

3. illustrating their use by applying the indicators/metrics in the context of some real-world DLs (e.g., ACM DL, CITIDEL [28], NDLTD [26, 72]).

Table 1.2 connects the proposed dimensions with some 'S'-related concepts involved in their definition. In the same way that the formalized 5S model helps to precisely define the higher-level DL concepts used here, we will use these formalizations to help define the quality indicators and their corresponding computations.

1.4 DIGITAL OBJECTS

1.4.1 ACCESSIBILITY

A digital object is accessible by a DL actor or patron, if it exists in the repository of the DL, a service is able to retrieve the object, and: (1) an overly restrictive rights management property of a metadata specification does not exist for that object; or (2) if such exists, the property does not restrict access for the particular society to which the actor belongs or to that actor in particular. A quality indicator for calculating accessibility is a function, which depends on all those factors and the granularity of the rules (e.g., entire object, structured streams). It should be noted that digital object accessibility as defined here is different from the common view of "website accessibility," which is concerned with creating better ways to provide Web content to users with disabilities [93]. For reasons of space we omit discussion of indicators associated with that type of accessibility.

Let *access constraint* be a property of some metadata specification of a digital object do_x whose values include the sets of communities that have the right to access specific (structured) streams within the object. Also let $struct\_streams(do_x) = \Omega_x$ be the set of structured streams of do_x. The accessibility $acc(do_x, ac_y)$ of a digital object do_x to an actor ac_y is:

- 0, if there is no collection C in the DL repository R such that $do_x \in C$;

- otherwise $acc = (\sum_{z \in struct\_streams(do_x)} r_z(ac_y))/|struct\_streams(do_x)|$, where:

  $r_z(ac_y)$ is a rights management rule defined as an indicator function:

  1, if

  > **structured stream** z has no access constraints; or
  >
  > **structured stream** z has access constraints and $ac_y \in cm_z$, where $cm_z \in Soc(1)$ is a community that has the right to access z; and

  0, otherwise.

Note that in the above definition, we chose to use a fine-grained granularity in the level of structured streams, allowing cases where specific parts of a digital object may be restricted (e.g., a chapter or a figure) and others not. In this definition accessibility is always in the [0,1] range. Note also that, from a broader perspective, the accessibility of a given digital object could be affected,

Table 1.1: DL high-level concepts and corresponding DL dimensions of quality with respective metrics

DL Concept	Dimension of Quality	Factors/Variables Involved in Measuring
Digital object	Accessibility	Collection, # of structured streams, rights management metadata, communities
	Pertinence	Context, information, information need
	Preservability	Fidelity (lossiness), migration cost, digital object complexity, stream formats
	Relevance	Query (representation), digital object (representation), external judgment
	Similarity	Same as in relevance, plus: citation/link patterns
	Significance	Citation/link patterns
	Timeliness	Age, time of latest citation, collection freshness
Metadata specification	Accuracy	Accurate attributes, # of attributes in the record
	Completeness	Missing attributes, schema size
	Conformance	Conformant attributes, schema size
Collection	Completeness	Collection size, size of the 'ideal collection'
Catalog	Completeness	# of digital objects without a set of metadata specifications, size of the described collection
	Consistency	# of sets of metadata specifications per digital object
Repository	Completeness	# of collections
	Consistency	# of collections in repository, catalog/collection pairwise consistency
Services	Composability	Extensibility, Reusability
	Efficiency	Response time
	Effectiveness	Precision/recall (search), F1 measure (classification)
	Extensibility	# of extended services, # of services in the DL, # of lines of code per service manager
	Reusability	# of reused services, # of services in the DL, # of lines of code per service manager
	Reliability	# of service failures, # of accesses

Table 1.2: Dimensions of quality and Ss involved in their definitions

DL Concept	Dimension of Quality	Some 'S' Concepts Involved
Digital object	Accessibility	Societies (actor), Structures (metadata specification), Streams + Structures (structured streams)
	Pertinence	Societies (actor), Scenarios (task)
	Preservability	Streams, Structures (structural metadata), Scenarios (process (e.g., migration))
	Relevance	Streams + Structures (structured streams), Structures (query), Spaces (Metric, Probabilistic, Vector)
	Similarity	Same as in relevance, plus: Structures (citation/link patterns)
	Significance	Structures (citation/link patterns)
	Timeliness	Streams (time), Structures (citation/link patterns)
Metadata specification	Accuracy	Structure (properties, values)
	Completeness	Structure (properties, schema)
	Conformance	Structure (properties, schema)
Collection	Completeness	Structure (collection)
Catalog	Completeness	Structure (collection)
	Consistency	Structure (collection)
Repository	Completeness	Structure (collection)
	Consistency	Structure (catalog, collection)
Services	Composability	see Extensibility, Reusability
	Efficiency	Streams (time), Spaces (operations, contraints)
	Effectiveness	see Pertinence, Relevance
	Extensibility	Societies + Scenarios (extends, inherits from, redefines)
	Reusability	Societies + Scenarios (includes, reuses)
	Reliability	Societies + Scenarios (uses, executes, invokes)

not only by rights management, but also by technological constraints, such as the lack of Acrobat Reader to open a full-text paper in PDF format, temporary network disconnection, or restriction on the number of simultaneous users, etc. In this work we have tried to focus on easily measurable intrinsic properties of the objects themselves and of the relationships between the actor and the objects. Finally, the accessibility of a digital object is always time-dependent as specific temporal embargoes may be imposed or removed.

Example of use. At Virginia Tech, a student can choose, at the moment of submission, to allow her electronic thesis or dissertation (ETD) to be viewed: worldwide, by those at the originating university, or not at all (e.g., when a patent will be applied for soon). The "mixed" case occurs when some portions (e.g., particular chapters or multimedia files) have restricted access while others are more widely available. The majority of Virginia Tech students choose their documents to be viewable worldwide, eventually; some initially choose not to grant worldwide access because of concerns regarding publication of results in journals/conferences.

Therefore, the accessibility $acc(etd_x, ac_y)$ of a Virginia Tech ETD etd_x is:

- 0, if etd_x does not belong to the VT-ETD collection;

- otherwise $(\sum_{z \in struct\_streams(etd_x)} r_z(ac_y))/|struct\_streams(etd_x)|$, where:

    $r_z(ac_y)$ is a rights management rule defined as an indicator function:

        1, if

            etd_x is marked as "worldwide access" or

            etd_x is marked as "VT only" and $ac_y \in VT_{cmm}$, where VT_{cmm} is the community of Virginia Tech ID holders accessing z through a computer with a Virginia Tech registered IP address.

        0, otherwise.

Table 1.3 shows a partial view as of March 25, 2003 of the number of ETDs that were: unrestricted (worldwide, accessibility = 1 to everybody), restricted to the VT campus (accessibility = 0 worldwide, 1 to members of VT_{cmm}), or mixed, along with the degree of accessibility $acc(etd_x, ac_y)$ of the mixed ETDs for non-VT_{cmm} members ac_y. For example, five out of the six chapters (structured streams) of the third mixed ETD under the letter A were available only to VT. The rights management

Table 1.3: Accessibility of VT-ETDs (first column corresponds to the first letter of the author's last name)

First letter of author's name	Unrestricted	Restricted	Mixed	Degree of accessibility for users not in the VT community
A	164	50	5	mix(0.5, 0.5, 0.167, 0.1875, 0.6)
B	286	102	3	mix(0.5,0.5, 0.13)
C	231	108	7	mix (0.11, 0.5, 0.5, 0.5, 0.33, 0.09, 0.33)
D	159	54	2	mix(0.875, 0.666)
E	67	26	1	mix(0.5)

rule therefore is 0 for all those chapters, thus making its overall accessibility to non-VT actors 1/6 or 0.167. Note that accessibility for the Virginia Tech ETDs has improved since 2003; indicators like this may be of help for those who work on collection development policies.

1.4.2   PERTINENCE

Pertinence is one of the most "social" quality indicators since it is a relation between the information carried by a digital object and an actor's information need. It depends heavily on the actor's knowledge, background, current task, etc.

Let $Inf(do_i)$ represent the "information"[6] (not physical) carried by a digital object do_i in any of its components, $IN(ac_j)$ be the information need[7] of an actor ac_j, and $Context(ac_j, k)$ be an amalgam of societal factors that affect the judgment of pertinence of do_i by ac_j at time k.[8] These include, among others, task, time, place, the actor's history of interaction, and a range of other factors that are not given explicitly but are implicit in the interaction and ambient environment. A complete formalization of context is out of the scope of this work. The reader is referred to a workshop on "Context in Information Retrieval" for a number of papers on the subject [49].

Also, we define, for future reference, two time-dependent sub-communities of actors, *users*, and *external-judges* $\subset Ac$, as:

- *users*: set of actors with an information need who use DL services to try to fulfill/satisfy that need,

- *external-judges*: set of actors responsible for determining the relevance (see Section 1.4.4) of a document to a query. We also assume that an external-judge can not be assigned to judge the relevance of a document to a query representing her own information need, i.e., at each point in time $users \cap external\text{-}judges = \emptyset$.

The pertinence of a digital object do_i to a user ac_j at a time k is an indicator function[9] $Pertinence(do_i, ac_j, k) : Inf(do_i) \times IN(ac_j) \times Context(ac_j, k)$ defined as:

- 1, if $Inf(do_i)$ is judged by ac_j to be informative with regards to $IN(ac_j)$ in context $Context(ac_j, k)$;

- 0, otherwise.

Values of pertinence function can be binary, or in range [0,1], depending on whether we give a degree, or just have a decision based on some threshold. We adopt the binary version here. This

---

[6]Information and information need, by themselves, are hard notions to formally define. One comprehensive attempt is presented in [70].

[7]Certain authors such as Taylor [113] and Mizzaro [71] make a distinction between the "real" and the "perceived" information need. We will not make this distinction here, in the interest of brevity.

[8]We consider if any part of do_i is pertinent at time k to actor ac_j's information need.

[9]We agree with Voorhees [119], Greisdorf [42], and others who argue for non-binary pertinence/relevance functions, but such is not normal practice. We will leave extensions to our definitions for these cases for future work.

coarse or macro view of pertinence could be supplemented by a similar definition of "full-pertinence" which would require that pertinence be assessed with respect to the full or entire document, do_i, and thus be stricter, taking an "all of" perspective, instead of our "any part of" perspective. Since pertinence is a subjective judgment made by a user in a particular context it can ultimately only be assessed by the user herself.

1.4.3   PRESERVABILITY

Preservability is a quality property of a digital object that reflects a state of the object that can vary due to changes in hardware (e.g., new recording technologies), software (e.g., release of a new version of the software used to create/display the object), representation formats (e.g., image standard such as JPEG 2000), and processes to which the object is submitted (e.g., migration).

There are four main technical approaches to digital preservation:

1. Migration: transforming from one digital format to another format, normally a successive subsequent one (e.g., from JPEG to JPEG 2000) [17].

2. Emulation: re-creating the original operating environment by saving the original programs and or creating new programs that can emulate the old environment [92].

3. Wrapping: packaging the object to be preserved with enough human readable metadata to allow it to be decoded in the future [121].

4. Refreshing: copying the stream of bits from one location to another, whether the physical medium is the same or not [64].

Note that here we are not considering physical deterioration of the medium in which the object is stored, since this is a property of the medium itself, not the object. However, we acknowledge that this is an important problem, for which "refreshing" is the normally used approach.

For cost, operational, and technical reasons, migration is the most widely used of the three techniques mentioned above [121]. However, the ideal solution should be some combination of all the techniques [47, 121]. One example that applies to such a combination is the UVC-based approach [66]. Nonetheless, for the purpose of the discussion below, we will concentrate on migration issues.

A digital object's preservability can be affected by its obsolescence and the fidelity of the migration process (see Figure 1.1). Obsolescence reflects the fact that a very obsolete object is really hard and costly to migrate, given the difficulty of finding appropriate migration tools and the right expertise. Fidelity reflects the differences between the original and the migrated object or, in other words, reflects the distortion or the loss of information inherent in the migration process that is absorbed by the object. The more obsolete the object, and the less faithful the migration process, the lower the object's preservability. Preservability also is affected by contextual issues of specific DLs. For example, while it is desirable to always use the most faithful migration process, a DL custodian may not have sufficient resources (money, storage, personnel) to apply that process to digital objects during migration. Based on the above discussion and on the fact that these two factors are orthogonal, we can define the preservability of a digital object do_i in a digital library dl as a tuple:

$$preservability(do_i, dl) = (\textit{fidelity of migrating}(do_i, format_x, format_y), \qquad (1.1)$$
$$obsolescence(do_i, dl)).$$

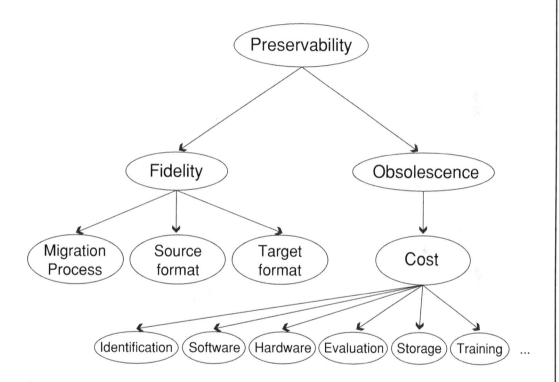

Figure 1.1: Factors in preservability (all links should be assumed to have "depends on" as their labels).

As mentioned before, obsolescence is a complex notion to capture, depending on many contextual factors. Since the choice of how to deal with obsolescence generally depends on resources at the disposal of the DL custodian, one possible idea is to approximate its value by using the actual cost of migrating the object [95]. While a complete cost model for preservability/obsolescence is beyond the scope of this work, we recognize many factors that can affect the cost, including:

- capital direct costs:

    - software development/acquiring or license updating for newer versions, and

    - hardware (for preservation processing or storage);

- indirect operating costs:

    - identifying candidate digital objects,

    - evaluating/examining/negotiating intellectual property issues and rights,

    - storage, and

    - staff training (on software/procedures).

Obsolescence then can be defined as *obsolescence*(do_i, dl) = cost of converting/migrating the digital object do_i within the context of the specific digital library dl.

The fidelity of the migration process p of a digital object do_i from *format*$_x$ to *format*$_y$ can be defined based on the inverse of the distortion or noise introduced by the migration process mp, i.e.,

$$fidelity(do_i, format_x, format_y) = \frac{1}{distortion(mp(format_x, format_y)) + 1.0}.$$

Distortion can be computed in a number of ways depending on the type of object and transformation [101]. One very common measure, when converting between similar formats, is the *mean squared error (mse)*. In the case of a digital object, *mse* can be defined as follows. Let $\{x_n\}$ be a stream of a digital object do_i and $\{y_n\}$ be the converted/migrated stream; the mean squared error $mse(\{x_n\}, \{y_n\}) = \frac{1}{N} * \sum_{n=1}^{N}(x_n - y_n)^2$, where N is the size of each stream. The average mean square error for the whole object do_i can be calculated as the average of *mse* for all its streams. This assumes that the other components (graphs and functions) of a digital object will be converted exactly.

Example of Use. Let us consider the following scenario adapted from [47]. In 2004, a librarian receives an email notifying her that a special collection[10] of 1,000 digital images, stored in TIFF version 5.0, is in danger of becoming obsolete, due to the fact that the latest version of the display software no longer supports TIFF 5.0. The librarian decides to migrate all digital photos to JPEG 2000, which now has become the *de facto* image preservation standard, recommended by the Research Libraries Group (RLG) [47].

The librarian does a small search for possible migration options and finds a tool, costing $500, which converts TIFF 5.0 directly to JPEG 2000. Let us consider that the amount of time taken by the librarian and the system administrator to order the software, install it, learn it, and apply it to all digital images combined takes 20 hours. Assume also that the hourly rate in this library is $66.60 per hour per employee.[11] In order to save space, the librarian chooses to use in the migration a compression rate which produces an average *mse* of 8 per image. In this scenario, the preservability of each digital image would correspond to: preservability (image-TIFF 5.0, dl) = (1/9, ($500 + $66.60 * 20) /1000) = (0.11, $1.83).

---

[10]Preservation of a collection, instead of a digital object, also may involve preserving all the structures (e.g., classification schemes, etc.) imposed on the collection.

[11]1800 is the number of hours in a work-year (37.5 hrs/wk * 48 wks/yr) and $110,000 the total annual cost of an employee working for this DL, based on salary, benefits, and expenses.

Note that although the example focuses on the obsolescence component of the indicator, we are not arguing by any means that it is less or more important than the "fidelity of migrating" component, since they capture different but complementary aspects of the preservability of a digital object. For instance, the obsolescence may not be high but if the migration process looses or distorts most of the actual information carried by the object for some specific purposes (e.g., image analysis), the overall preservability is low. This is the main reason why we decided not to combine into a single indicator the two aspects that characterize preservability.

1.4.4   RELEVANCE

A digital object is *relevant* [96] in the context of an expression of an information need (e.g., a query) or interest (e.g., profile) and a service (e.g., searching, recommending). A role of an information satisfaction service is to provide ways to find the most relevant information for the user, which in the case of DLs is carried by digital objects and their metadata specifications.

The relevance of a digital object to a query is an indicator function $Relevance(do_i, q)$ defined as:

- 1, if do_i is considered by an *external-judge* to be relevant to q;

- 0, otherwise.

Values of relevance can be binary, or in range $[0,1]$, depending on whether we give a degree, or just have a decision based upon some threshold. We adopt the binary version here. The most common measures for relevance estimates/predictions are based on statistical properties of the streams of the digital object and the queries. For example, in the vector space model, relevance is estimated based on the distance between the vectors representing the objects and queries (as measured by the angle between them), and the components of these vectors are derived from values such as frequency of a term in a document, the frequency of the term in the collection, document size, document structure, query size, collection size, etc. Note that, in contrast to pertinence, relevance is a relation between a representation of a document and a representation of an information need (i.e., query). Also, it is supposed to be an objective, public, and social notion that can be established by a general consensus in the field, not a subjective, private judgment between the actor and her information need [23, 54].

The distinction we have made between pertinence and relevance is derived from a view held by part of the information science community [15, 23, 54, 96, 97]. We have just formalized the two notions in the context of our framework. In Saracevic's work, for example, relevance, as defined by us, is called systemic or algorithmic relevance, and is a relationship between a text and a query. Pertinence, or cognitive relevance, is a relationship between the state of knowledge and cognitive information need of a user and the objects retrieved. Cognitive correspondence, informativeness, novelty, information quality, and the like are criteria by which cognitive relevance is inferred.

The external-judges should evaluate the relevance of the object to the query without the cognitive load resulting from contextual interference, therefore their judgments should be more objective and more generally applicable.

1.4.5   SIGNIFICANCE

Significance of a digital object can be viewed from two perspectives: (1) relative to its pertinence or relevance, or (2) in absolute terms, irrespective of particular user requirements. Absolute significance can be calculated based on *raw citedness*—-the number of times a document do_i is cited, or the frequency of occurrence of citations whose target is do_i. Other factors may play a role in the significance of a document such as the prestige of the journal publishing the work, its use in courses, awards given, etc., but these are very hard to quantify/measure. For the sake of brevity and simplicity, therefore, we focus on raw citedness, though various alternatives or complementary measures might be employed, e.g., (1) number of downloads (adjusted to account for robots and spam), (2) rate of citation (over some time period of interest, or normalized based on history), (3) pagerank (or similar measure of popularity and/or importance), or (4) values from hub/authority computations.

Example of Use. We used 98,000 documents from the ACM Digital Library,[12] which corresponded to approximately 1,093,700 (outgoing) citations (average of 11.53 citations per document). Table 1.4 shows the top five documents in the ACM collection with the highest values of significance.

Table 1.4: Documents with the highest degree of significance			
Document	Publication	Year	Significance
Computer programming as art	CACM	1974	279
A generalized processor sharing approach to flow control in integrated services networks: the single-node case	IEEE/ACM Transactions on Networking (TON)	1993	138
The entity-relationship model – toward a unified view of data	ACM Transactions on Database Systems	1976	130
A relational model of data for large shared data banks	CACM	1970	121
Revised report on the algorithmic language scheme	ACM SIGPLAN Notices	1986	116

Note that significance, as defined, is supposed to increase with time, as more people take notice of the work and acknowledge it through citations. As such, publication date affects this indicator (and timeliness, see below, as well) since older publications have more chance of being cited.

1.4.6   SIMILARITY

Similarity metrics reflect the relatedness between two or more digital objects. An object similar to another relevant or pertinent object has a good chance of also having these properties, but an object *too* similar to another supposedly different object can reveal a lack of quality (e.g., plagiarism, which might be found through plagiarism software) unless it is a variant version which can be identified through a de-duping process.

Similarity can be measured based on the digital object's content (streams) (e.g., use and frequency of words), digital object's internal organization (structures), or patterns of citations/links. For example, similarity between two documents can be calculated using the cosine distance between the vectors representing the documents [7]. This idea can be expanded to calculate similarity between corresponding structured streams of documents (e.g., using their title and abstract texts). Other measures, such as "bag-of-words" and Okapi can be used to calculate similarity as well [7].

---

[12]Thanks go to ACM for allowing us access to this 2002 data in connection with our related work on the CITIDEL project.

Similarity measures also may use link or citation information to compute the relatedness of two objects. Among the most popular citation-based measures of similarity are: co-citation [107], bibliographic coupling [55], and the Amsler measure. The last one is a combination of the previous two, so we will explain only the Amsler measure [4].

According to Amsler, two documents d_i and d_j are related if (1) d_i and d_j are cited by the same document, (2) d_i and d_j cite the same document, or (3) d_i cites a third document d_k that cites d_j. Thus, let Pd_i be the set of parents of d_i, and let Cd_i be the set of children of d_i. The Amsler similarity between two pages d_i and d_j is defined as:

$$Amsler(d_i, d_j) = \frac{|(Pd_i \cup Cd_i) \cap (Pd_j \cup Cd_j)|}{max(|Pd_i \cup Cd_i|, |Pd_j \cup Cd_j|)}.$$ (1.2)

Eq. 1.2 tells us that, the more links (either parents or children) d_i and d_j have in common, the more they are related. The absolute Amsler degree of a document d_i in collection C is defined as $\sum_{d_j \in C - \{d_i\}} Amsler(d_i, d_j)$.

Example of use. Table 1.5 shows the top five documents in the ACM collection we studied with the highest absolute values of Amsler.

Table 1.5: Documents with the highest absolute Amsler degree

Document	Publication	Year	Amsler
Computer programming as an art	CACM	1974	69.15
Compiler transformations for high-performance computing	CSUR	1994	64.31
Analysis of pointers and structures	Prog. language design and implementation	1990	62.56
Query evaluation techniques for large databases	CSUR	1993	59.81
A schema for interprocedural modification side-effect analysis with pointer aliasing	TOPLAS	2001	57.90

1.4.7 TIMELINESS

Timeliness of a digital object is the extent to which it is sufficiently up-to-date for the task at hand [80]. It can be a function of the time when the digital object was created, stored, accessed, or cited.

Since the timeliness of an object is directly related to the information it carries, which still can be timely even if the object is "old,"[13] a good quality indicator of this quality dimension is the time of the latest citation, since it's a measure that:

1. captures the fact that the information carried by the object is still relevant by the time the citing object was published;

2. is independent from the actor that receives the object and the time the object is delivered; and

3. reflects the overall importance of the object inside its community of interest.

[13] For instance, classics such as the Bible or writings of Plato may always be timely for some tasks.

As it is known that many documents are never cited, an alternative is to consider the age of the object itself. Therefore, the timeliness of a digital object do_i (which is best if zero) can be defined as:

- (current time or time of last freshening) - (time of the latest citation), if object is ever cited, otherwise as

- (current time or time of last freshening) - (creation time or publication time), if object is never cited.

Time of last freshening, which is defined as the time of the creation/publication of the most recent object in the collection to which do_i belongs,[14] may be used instead of current time if the collection is not updated frequently.

Example of use. Figure 1.2 shows the distribution of timeliness (0 through 10) for documents in the ACM DL with citations. Time of last freshening is 2002. It can be seen, discounting the first set of values (timeliness=0), that there is an inverse relation between timeliness and the size of the set of documents with that value: the smaller the value, the bigger the set, meaning that as time passes there is less chance that a document will be cited.

1.5   METADATA SPECIFICATIONS AND METADATA FORMAT

Three main dimensions of quality can be associated with metadata specifications and metadata formats: accuracy, completeness, and conformance.

1.5.1   ACCURACY

Accuracy is defined in terms of properties of a metadata specification for a digital object. Accuracy of a triple (r, p, v) (i.e., $(resource, property, {}^{15}value)$) refers to the nearness of the value v to some value v' in the attribute range that is considered the correct one for the (resource, property) pair (r, p) [91]. Note that in 5S, a metadata specification (Def. MI B.13 in Book 1) is defined as a structure (G, L, F), G being a graph, L a set of labels, and F a labelling function associating components (i.e., nodes and vertices) of the graph with labels. In other words, a metadata specification can be seen as a labeled digraph. The triple $st = (F(v_i), F(e), F(v_j))$ is called a statement (derived from the descriptive metadata specification), meaning that the resource labeled $F(v_i)$ has property or attribute $F(e)$ with value $F(v_j)$. A metadata specification for a digital object is completely accurate with respect to a digital object if all the (derived) triples are accurate, assuming some appropriate accuracy threshold. The degree of accuracy of triple (r, p, v) can be defined as an indicator function or with specific rules for a particular schema/catalog. It is dependent on several factors, including

---

[14]Our definition considers citations inside the collection, so adding a document to the collection that cites another also is a freshening.
[15]In this chapter we will use the terms 'metadata property', 'metadata attribute', and 'metadata field' interchangeably.

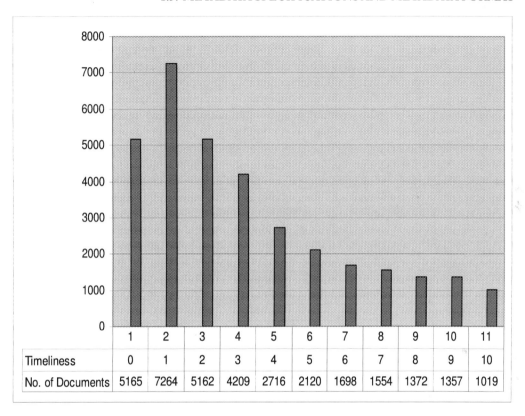

	1	2	3	4	5	6	7	8	9	10	11
Timeliness	0	1	2	3	4	5	6	7	8	9	10
No. of Documents	5165	7264	5162	4209	2716	2120	1698	1554	1372	1357	1019

Figure 1.2: Timeliness in the ACM Digital Library.

the attribute's range of values v, intended use, etc. Examples are given below. Thus, the degree of accuracy $acc(ms_x)$ of a metadata specification ms_x can be defined as

$$acc(ms_x) = \frac{\sum_{\forall (r, p, v) \text{ from } ms_x} \text{degree of accuracy of } (r, p, v)}{\text{total number of triples}(r, p, v) \text{ from } ms_x} \qquad (1.3)$$

Example of Use. To illustrate the application of such an indicator we used the NDLTD Union Catalog. We chose OCLC's version of the NDLTD Union Catalog[16] because of the numerous problems at the time regarding metadata accuracy, observed while creating a collection for filtering experiments [122]. For example, author information is very commonly found in the title field ("The concept of the church in the thought of Rudolf Bultmann—by Paul E. Stambach.") and sometimes

---

[16]This was before 2004; more recently the Union Catalog has been run from the University of Cape Town, but there still are data quality problems, since each site manages its own records.

the abstract contains all kinds of information (see below) but not the thesis/dissertation's summary. We defined the following rules for the dc.author,[17] dc.title, and dc.abstract fields.

- Degree of accuracy of $(*, dc.title, *)$ for the NDLTD Union Catalog = 1, if dc.title does not contain author information; 0.5 otherwise. In case it is empty or null it receives a 0 (zero) value.

- Degree of accuracy of $(*, dc.abstract, *)$ = 1 if the field corresponds to the thesis' or dissertation's summary; 0 otherwise. The decision of whether a dc.abstract field corresponds to a summary or not was based on the size of the text and a number of heuristics. For example, (1) if dc.abstract is equal to "Thesis" or "Dissertation," it is not a summary; (2) if dc.abstract contains phrases like "Title from *" (e.g., "Title from first page of PDF file"), "Document formatted into pages," "Includes bibliographical references," "Mode of access," among others, it is not a summary.

According to these two rules the average OCLC accuracy for all its metadata records (approximately 14,000 records, in September 2003[18]) was calculated as around 0.79, assuming a maximum of 1.

1.5.2   COMPLETENESS

Completeness is a pervasive quality dimension that is associated with many of the DL concepts. The general notion of completeness can be defined as: (number of units of a particular concept)/(ideal number of units of that concept). This notion can be adapted or instantiated for specific DL concepts.

Completeness of metadata specifications refers to the degree to which values are present in the description, according to a metadata standard. As far as an individual property is concerned, only two situations are possible: either a value is assigned to the property in question, or not. The degree of completeness of a metadata specification ms_x can be defined as[19]

$$Completeness(ms_x) = 1 - \frac{\text{no. of missing attributes in } ms_x}{\text{total no. of attributes in the schema for } ms_x} \tag{1.4}$$

Note that the assumption here is that the more complete, the better. However, we acknowledge that there can be situations, for example, determined on purpose in accordance with local needs, in which this is not always true.

Example of use. Figure 1.3 shows the average of completeness of all metadata specifications (records) in site catalogs of the NDLTD Union Catalog administered by OCLC as of February 23, 2004, relative to the Dublin Core metadata standard (15 attributes).

---

[17]The author field in the Dublin Core standard.
[18]Over 250K in Nov. 2006, over 1.8M in Nov. 2010, and approximately 3M in early 2013.
[19]According to the definition of completeness in [36].

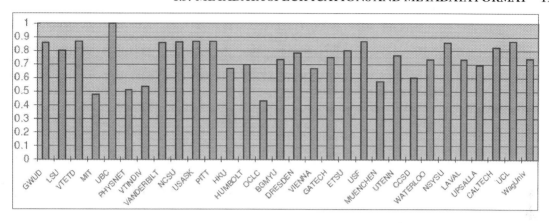

Figure 1.3: Average completeness of site catalogs in the NDLTD Union Catalog (as of February 2004).

1.5.3   CONFORMANCE

The conformance of a metadata specification to a metadata standard/format/schema has been formally defined in Def. MI B.16 in Book 1. In that definition a value of an attribute is conformant to its schema if it has the data type of the attribute (e.g., string, date, number, etc.). That definition can be extended to include cardinality (i.e., considering mandatory/optional fields) and multiplicity (i.e., considering repeatable fields) issues.

A metadata specification ms_x is *cardinally conformant* to a metadata format if:

1. it conforms with its schema in terms of the data types of its attributes according to Def. MI B. 14 in Book 1.

2. each attribute att_{xy} of ms_x appears at least once if att_{xy} is marked as mandatory in the schema; and

3. att_{xy} does not appear more than once if it is not marked as repeatable in the schema.

From now on, we will use conformance to refer to the stronger definition of *cardinally conformant*. Different from completeness, an attribute may be missing in a metadata specification, but the attribute still can be considered conformant, if it is not marked as mandatory in the mandatory schema. The degree of conformance of a metadata specification ms_x can be defined as

$$\text{Conformance}(ms_x) = \frac{\displaystyle\sum_{\text{attributes } att_{xy} \text{ in schema } ms_x} \text{degree of conformance of } att_{xy}}{\text{total number of attributes in the schema for } ms_x}. \quad (1.5)$$

The degree of conformance of att_{xy} is an indicator function defined as 1 if att_{xy} obeys all conditions specified in the above definition; 0 otherwise.

Example of use. Figure 1.4 shows the average conformance of the metadata records in the site catalogs of the NDLTD Union Catalog, relative to the ETD-MS metadata standard for electronic theses and dissertations.[20] ETD-MS, different from the Dublin Core in which all fields are optional, defines six mandatory fields: dc.title, dc.creator, dc.subject, dc.date, dc.type, dc.identifier. Also, the range for the dc.type is defined as the set {'Collection', 'Dataset', 'Event', 'Image','InteractiveResource', 'Software', 'Sound', 'Text', 'PhysicalObject', 'StillImage', 'MovingImage', 'Electronic Thesis or Dissertation'}. If any value other than these words/phrases is used for the attribute, it is defined as non-conformant.

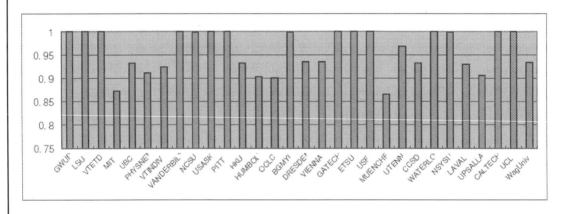

Figure 1.4: Average conformance of site catalogs in the NDLTD Union Catalog.

1.6   COLLECTION, METADATA CATALOG, AND REPOSITORY

1.6.1   COLLECTION COMPLETENESS

A complete DL collection is one which contains all the existing digital objects that it should hold. Measuring completeness of a collection can be extremely hard or virtually impossible in many cases when there is no way to determine the ideal real-world collection such as in the Web or in hidden databases. Advanced judicious sampling or probing of alternative repositories whose completeness has been established manually can give crude estimates [51]. An example could be to approximate a measure of the completeness of a computer science collection of papers on a specific topic by sampling the ACM or IEEE-CS digital libraries, DBLP, and some other commercial publishers' on-line databases. In other cases such as for harvested or mirrored collections those estimates are easier to establish. More formally, Completeness(C_x) of a collection C_x, can be defined as the ratio

---

[20]http://www.ndltd.org/standards/metadata/etd-ms-v1.1.html

between the size of C_x and the ideal real-world collection, i.e.,

$$Completeness(C_x) = \frac{|C_x|}{|\text{ideal collection}|}.$$
(1.6)

Example of use. The ACM Guide is a collection of bibliographic references and abstracts of works published by ACM and other publishers. The Guide can be considered a good approximation of an ideal computing collection for a number of reasons, including the fact that it contains most of the different types of computing-related literature and for each type it can be considered fairly complete. For example, in 2004, the set of theses in the Guide came from Proquest-UMI, which receives copies of almost all dissertations defended in the U.S. or Canada; the number of technical reports was close to that managed by NCSTRL, the largest repository of CS technical reports, and it contains large numbers of records from many of the most important publishers in computer science (such as ACM, IEEE, Springer, and Elsevier). Table 1.6 shows the degree of completeness of several CS-related collections[21] when compared with the Guide.

Table 1.6: Completeness of several collections

Collection	Degree of Completeness
ACM Guide	1
DBLP	0.652
CITIDEL(DBLP(partial) + ACM(partial) + NCSTRL + NDLTD-CS)	0.467
IEEE-DL	0.168
ACM-DL	0.146

1.6.2 CATALOG COMPLETENESS AND CONSISTENCY

The degree of completeness of a catalog DM_C for a collection C can be defined accordingly as

$$Completeness(DM_C) = 1 - \frac{\text{no. of } do\text{'s} \in C \text{ without a metadata specification}}{\text{size of the collection C}}.$$
(1.7)

Since each object is unique by nature (e.g., each has a unique global handle) two different objects should not have the same metadata description. A catalog in which this occurs is therefore considered inconsistent. It should be noted, though, that an object can have more than one metadata specification (e.g., a Dublin Core and a MARC one).

Consistency, accordingly, is an indicator function defined as

- 0, if there is at least one set of metadata specifications assigned to more than one digital object;

- 1, otherwise.

Example of use. In April 2004, the NDLTD Union Catalog administered by OCLC tried to harvest data from the Brazilian Digital Library of Electronic Theses and Dissertations (BDTD). Because of problems in BDTD's implementation of the OAI protocol and problems with the Latin

---

[21] All of which are subsets of the Guide. Size of the Guide = 735,429 (as of March, 2004).

character set handling by OCLC, only 103 records were harvested from the repository. The BDTD collection contained 4446 records. Therefore, the completeness of the harvested catalog for BDTD in the Union Catalog would be completeness(BDTD in Union Catalog) = 1 - (4446 - 103)/4446 = 0.023. Note that completeness significantly improved by 2006.

1.6.3   REPOSITORY COMPLETENESS AND CONSISTENCY

A repository is complete if it contains all collections it should have. The degree of completeness of a repository R is defined as

$$Completeness(R) = \frac{\text{number of collections in the repository}}{\text{ideal number of collections}}. \tag{1.8}$$

If the repository stores collections with their respective metadata catalogs, its consistency can be defined in terms of these two components. Therefore, repository consistency is an indicator function defined as

- 1, if the consistency of all catalogs with respect to their described collections is 1;

- 0, otherwise.

Example of use. We will use the ACM Guide as the ideal collection. Not considering the Bibliography and Play subcollections of the Guide and considering each publisher as a different subcollection, the completeness of CITIDEL can be calculated as 4 (ACM + IEEE + NCTRL + NDLTD-CS) / 11 (total number of collections) or 0.36.

1.7   DL SERVICES

Dimensions of quality for DL services can be classified as external or internal [120]. The external view is related to information satisfaction services and is concerned with the use and perceived value of these services from the point of view of societies of end users. The internal view addresses the construction and operation necessary to attain the required functionality, given a set of requirements that reflect the external view. Issues in system construction, operation, design, and implementation should be considered.

1.7.1   EFFECTIVENESS AND EFFICIENCY

The two most obvious external quality indicators of DL services, as perceived by end users, are efficiency and effectiveness. Efficiency is most commonly measured in terms of speed, i.e., the difference between request and response time. More formally, let $t(e)$ be the time of an event e, and let e_{ix} and e_{fx} be the initial and the final events of scenario sc_x in service Se. The efficiency of service Se is defined as

$$\text{Efficiency}(Se) = \frac{1}{max_{sc_x \in Se} (t(e_{fx}) - t(e_{ix})) + 1.0}. \tag{1.9}$$

Effectiveness is normally related to information satisfaction services and can be measured by batch experiments with test collections or through experiments with real users. Different types of information services can use different metrics, the most common ones being precision and recall [7], extensively deployed to assess quality of searching or filtering services.

1.7.2   EXTENSIBILITY AND REUSABILITY

Regarding design and implementation of DL services, there are two main classes of quality properties: (1) those regarding composability of services; and (2) those regarding qualitative aspects of the models and implementations. The latter include issues such as completeness, consistency, correctness, and soundness. We concentrate on composability aspects but acknowledge the importance and complexity of the other issues.

Composability can be defined in terms of reusability and extensibility. In short, a service Y *reuses* a service X if the behavior of Y incorporates the behavior of X (in the sense that scenarios of X also are scenarios of Y). A service Y *extends* a service X if it subsumes the behavior of X and potentially includes additional conditional subflows of events (the scenarios of X are subsequences of the scenarios of Y). A composed service either extends or reuses another service. A composable service (i.e., a service that can be extended or reused) has to satisfy a number of requirements including exporting clear interfaces, providing mechanisms/protocols for connections and passing of parameters, offering gateway or mediator services to convert between disparate document formats and protocols, and satisfying circumstantial conditions such as satisfaction of any pre-condition based on the service's current state and input values to any called service. All of these make it very hard to quantify the composability of a service. However, even if an indicator of composability can be determined, a service is still only potentially reusable and extensible. One more pragmatic indicator of the actual composability is to ascertain from a set of services and service managers that run or implement those services, which managers are actually inherited from or included by others. Therefore, given a set of services $Serv$ and a set of service managers SM that run those services, two quality indicators of extensibility and reusability can be defined.

- Macro-Extensibility(Serv) = $\dfrac{\sum\limits_{Se_i \in Serv} extended(Se_i)}{|Serv|}$, where $Serv$ is the set of services of the DL and $extended(Se_i)$ is an indicator function defined as

    1, if $\exists Se_j \in Serv : Se_j$ extends Se_i;

    0, otherwise.

- Micro-Extensibility(Serv) $= \dfrac{\sum\limits_{sm_x \in SM, Se_i \in Serv} LOC(sm_x) * extended(Se_i)}{\sum_{sm \in SM} LOC(sm)}$, where LOC corresponds to the number of lines of code of all operations of a service manager, and sm_x *runs* Se_i.

- Since reuse/inclusion has a different semantics of extension, reusability can accordingly be defined as Macro-Reusability(Serv) $= \dfrac{\sum\limits_{Se_i \in Serv} reused(Se_i)}{|Serv|}$, where $reused(Se_i)$ is an indicator function defined as

    1, if $\exists Se_j \in Serv : Se_j$ reuses Se_i;

    0, otherwise.

- Micro-Reusability(Serv) $= \dfrac{\sum\limits_{sm_x \in SM, Se_i \in Serv} LOC(sm_x) * reused(Se_i)}{\sum_{sm \in SM} LOC(sm)}$, where LOC corresponds to the number of lines of code of all operations of a service manager and sm_x *runs* Se_i.

Example of use. Table 1.7 shows the lines of code (LOC) needed to implement service managers that run several services in the ETANA archaeological digital library [89, 104, 106], in September, 2004 [87]. Let's assume a 1:1 ratio between the set of services and set of service managers. Reused services (and included service managers) are implemented as ODL components [108]. These services are searching, annotating, recommending, and (union) cataloging.

Table 1.7: Analysis of ETANA DL prototype using the metric of Lines of Code

Service	Component-based	LOC for implementing service	Total LOC	LOC reused from component
Searching back-end	Yes	-	1650	1650
Search wrapping	No	100	100	-
Recommending	Yes	-	700	700
Recommend wrapping	No	200	200	-
Annotating back-end	Yes	50	600	600
Annotate wrapping	No	50	50	-
Union catalog	Yes	-	680	680
User interface service	No	1800	1600	-
Browsing	No	1390	1390	-
Comparing (objects)	No	650	650	-
Marking items	No	550	550	-
Items of interest	No	480	480	-
Recent searches/discussions	No	230	230	-
Collections description	No	250	250	-
User management	No	600	600	-
Framework code	No	2000	2000	-
	Total	8280	11910	3630

The wrapping services, the ones that really reuse and provide the services offered by the DL components, are necessary in order to deal with issues such as invoking operations, parsing results, and interfacing with other components (like the user interface). However, the additional code for those wrappers is only a very small percentage of the total lines of code required for implementing the components. In the ETANA-DL prototype (in September, 2004), only a few important services were componentized and therefore reused (Macro-Reusability(ETANA DL Services)) = 4/16 =

0.25. However, Micro-Reusability = 3630/11910 = 0.304 makes it clear that we can re-use a very significant percentage of DL code by implementing common DL services as components. Moreover, as more service managers are componentized, more code and managers are potentially inherited from/included by more DLs.

1.7.3   RELIABILITY

Regarding DL operations, the most important quality criterion is reliability. Service reliability can be defined as the probability that the service will not fail during a given period of time [44]. We define the reliability of a service Se_x as

$$Reliability(Se_x) = 1 - \frac{\text{no. of failures}}{\text{no. of accesses}}. \tag{1.10}$$

A failure is characterized as an event that

1. was supposed to happen in a scenario but did not, or

2. did happen but did not execute some of its operations, or

3. did happen, where the operations were executed, but the results were not the correct ones.

Example of use. Table 1.8 shows reliability figures for the most popular services of CITIDEL, according to a log analysis done on April 1, 2004. The low reliability for the *structured searching* service can be explained by the fact that it was an experimental one, which ran only for a short period of time. However, entry points and links to this service were not removed after the experiments, and users kept using it without getting answers. This also shows how flaws in design can be found with such quality-oriented analysis.

Table 1.8: Reliability of CITIDEL services

CITIDEL service	No. of failures/No. of accesses	Reliability
Searching	73/14370	0.994
Browsing	4130/153369	0.973
Requesting (getobject)	1569/318036	0.995
Structured searching	214/752	0.66
Contributing	0/980	1

1.8   CASE STUDY: 5SQUAL

Digital libraries also may present many differences when compared or analyzed over time. The available content can grow in size and diversity. The provided services may exhibit changes in their usage patterns, their internal organization may evolve, etc. However, in practice, most DL evaluations occur only when a problem or situation that requires urgent intervention occurs. Those evaluations are usually very specific, depending on the particularities of each system. Thus, in order to improve development, which in the case of DLs is generally very expensive and time-consuming [108, 112], and to promote maintenance of such dynamic systems, periodic and recurrent quality assessments of the DL components should be performed.

With this goal in mind, we designed, implemented, and evaluated 5SQual, a tool intended for automatic quantitative evaluation of some of the most important components of a digital library, namely, digital objects, metadata, and services. 5SQual is grounded in a formal quality model for digital libraries [39]. The tool helps to manage and maintain digital libraries through automatic and recurrent evaluations that can diagnose problems and suggest possible improvements to the system, as well as demonstrate its evolution over time. Due to the complexity, heterogeneity, and diversity of DLs in terms of content and services, the tool has been designed to be flexible enough to be used by many different systems.

The potential applicability and usefulness of the tool was tested by employing it for the evaluation of real DLs, such as *Virginia Tech's Digital Library of Electronic Theses and Dissertations* (VT-ETD)[22] and *The Brazilian Digital Library of Computing* (BDBComp).[23] These evaluations generated information that, according to interviewed administrators, can be very useful to improve and maintain a DL. The tool and its evaluation serve also as a validation of the theoretical quality model for DLs presented in [39] and make it possible for DL administrators and digital librarians to apply the model in real settings. We also performed a usability study of the 5SQual interface with the help of usability specialists and conducted interviews with potential users (DL administrators). The results of both evaluations and the opinions expressed were in general very positive.

In sum, the main contributions of this work are: (1) the description of the design, architecture, implementation, and use of 5SQual, a tool for automatic quality assessment of digital libraries; (2) the evaluation (with usability specialists) of its graphical interface specially designed to guide the configuration of 5SQual evaluations; and (3) an analysis of the results of interviews discussing expectations regarding 5SQual, conducted with administrators of real DLs.

1.8.1 5SQUAL OVERVIEW

The construction of 5SQual was initially based on the implementation of a subset of the quality dimensions presented in Section 1.3. These dimensions were chosen for the first implementation of the tool because the respective numeric indicators are user independent and objective enough to allow an automatic evaluation. Other dimensions and numeric indicators can be added to the tool in the future.

The 5SQual Architecture

The 5SQual architecture was designed to allow the tool to be used by a large number of diverse DLs with different goals (e.g., complete periodical evaluations, diagnosis of problems). Since these systems

---

[22]http://scholar.lib.vt.edu/theses/.
[23]http://www.lbd.dcc.ufmg.br/bdbcomp/.

make the information necessary for evaluation available in many distinct ways, the architecture is flexible in several ways, including:

- Flexibility in data collection. Data for evaluation may be gathered from web pages, from the DL repositories via the Open Archives Protocol for Metadata Harvesting [73], or from the local filesystem.

- Flexibility in data extraction. Since the log files of a DL may use disparate formatting rules, the 5SQual architecture allows the user to utilize internal recognizers that come with the tool, for example, for the XMLLog format [38, 40], or to indicate specific external recognizers for a particular format.

- Flexibility in evaluation. The tool allows the user to specify which set of dimensions she wants to evaluate.

- Flexibility in utilization. 5SQual receives as input an XML file with the parameters necessary for retrieving and extracting the data for the calculation of the dimensions defined in an evaluation. To facilitate the construction of this input file, a special graphical user interface was implemented to guide the user throughout this configuration process in order to generate the file and call for the execution of the evaluation. It also is possible to generate only the configuration file and execute the evaluation later, via interface or via command line. The saved input file with all the configuration details also may be re-used in later evaluations.

Figure 1.5 shows the 5SQual architecture. The necessary information for the evaluation resides in the DL and should be retrieved through the DL application layer (e.g., through an OAI interface). The 5SQual architecture is organized as follows:

- Processing Layer: In this layer, we have three modules: the retrieval module, the extraction module, and the calculation module.

  - Retrieval module: This module is responsible for obtaining the necessary information for evaluation on the Web or in the local file system. It collects log files that record the behavior of the DL services, its digital objects, or metadata with information about these objects. For retrieving metadata on the Web, it uses the OAI interface. Digital objects and logs can be retrieved from the Web or from the local file system, through previously indicated file paths.

  - Extraction module: 5SQual uses parsers that have been specified by the user or the ones that already come with the tool. These parsers extract data from the collected files and convert them to the 5SQual standard formats that describe the necessary information for each dimension. The set of built-in parsers includes content parsers (e.g., for PDF and PS files), specific metadata format parsers (e.g., for Dublin Core and RFC1807 formats), and specific log format parsers (e.g., for the XMLLog format [38, 40]).

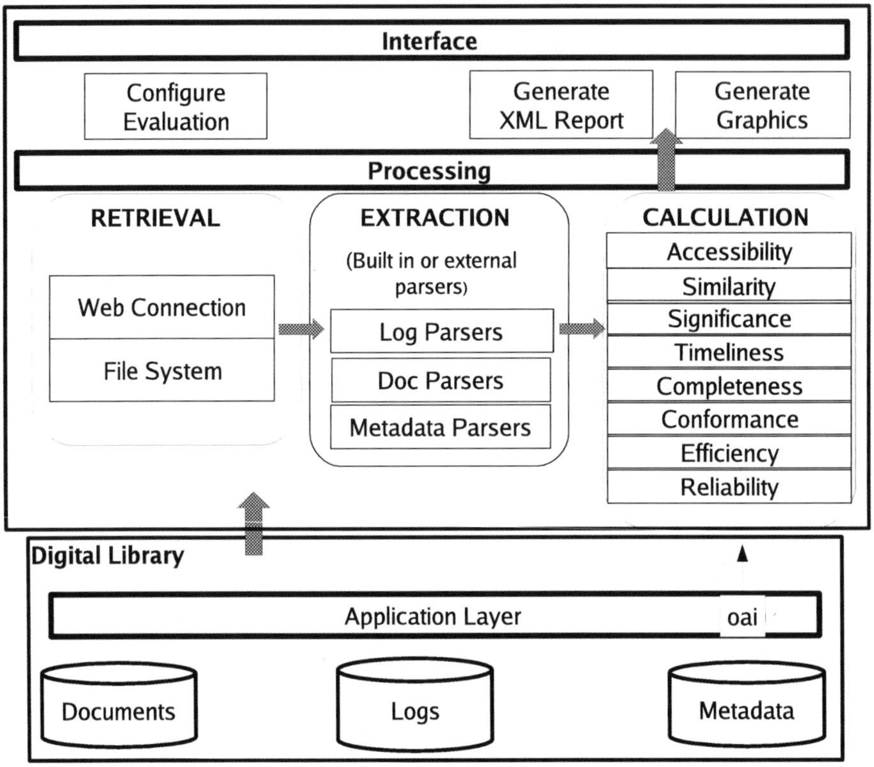

Figure 1.5: 5SQual architecture.

- Calculation module: In this module, 5SQual calculates a set of numeric indicators for each quality dimension.

- Interface Layer: The configuration module is responsible for storing the parameters defined for the evaluation. According to the choices made by the user, 5SQual generates XML reports and charts for each dimension, considering the evaluation results.

5SQual Operation

Before starting with 5SQual, a user, typically the administrator of a DL, has to configure the parameters for the evaluation through an interface that was specially developed to help with this task. The 5SQual interface works like a setup wizard that guides the user through the necessary configuration steps, assuring that the mandatory parameters have been filled before undertaking an evaluation. An XML file with the configured parameters is generated and can be imported later through the same interface to repeat the evaluation, making it easier for the user to analyze the system over time.

The parameters indicate where 5SQual should find information for the evaluation and how to extract them to calculate the selected dimensions. Once the documents, metadata, and any other necessary files are available, 5SQual extracts the required information. To accomplish this, 5SQual uses external programs specified by the user or the built-in parsers that come with the tool. Then, the extracted information is used to calculate numeric indicators for each dimension to be evaluated. In the following, we show a step-by-step configuration of an evaluation carried out using 5SQual.

The interface first presents to the user two options: (1) start a new evaluation from the beginning by following all the steps to configure the necessary parameters for this purpose, or (2) import a previously generated file with all the parameters already specified (see Figure 1.6).

If the user chooses to fill the parameters through the interface, she is then asked to identify this evaluation by giving the name of the DL that is being assessed and adding an optional description (see Figure 1.7). This serves to facilitate re-use of this configuration in a subsequent evaluation.

Next, the user must choose which quality dimensions to evaluate. The dimensions are selected from a set of checkboxes located in the left portion of the screen (see Figure 1.8). When a dimension is selected, the necessary resources for calculating the respective indicators are presented in the right portion of the screen. This is important to make the user aware of the resources that the DL must provide in order to be evaluated under that dimension. If this resource cannot be obtained, the dimension must be deselected. Another interesting aspect of the interface is the help icons (with the question marks) shown to the right of the name of each dimension. If the user presses one of these icons, a definition of the dimension along with the explanation of its numerical indicators is presented.

After choosing all the dimensions that will be evaluated, the user must configure the resources that are shown in the list on the right. For such, she must select in the list a specific resource and press the button *Configure Resource* (see Figure 1.8). That done, a window requesting information about where to retrieve the chosen resource pops up. In Figure 1.8, a configuration window of the resource of the dimension *Reliability* requests the path for the file containing data about the status of several DL service executions, during a period of time. The user can choose to look for this file in the local file system or remotely, on the Web. This resource is mandatory and must be configured before the user advances to the next step.

The user then must specify parameters about how to extract the data from the indicated resources and how to calculate the indicators for each selected dimension. In Figure 1.9, the dimensions chosen in the previous step are shown on the left portion of the screen. Once a dimension is selected, the area on the right changes, presenting a panel that requests information about the parameters for the selected dimension. In Figure 1.9, the user chose the dimension *Reliability* and configured the necessary parameter: the recognizer program used to extract information from the log file containing data about the status of the executions of the DL services. In that case, the user specified a resource to be parsed using the 5SQual plugin for the XMLLog format.

The user next must define which files the 5SQual tool will generate and where to save them, as shown in Figure 1.10. First, the user must define where to save the configuration file, which can

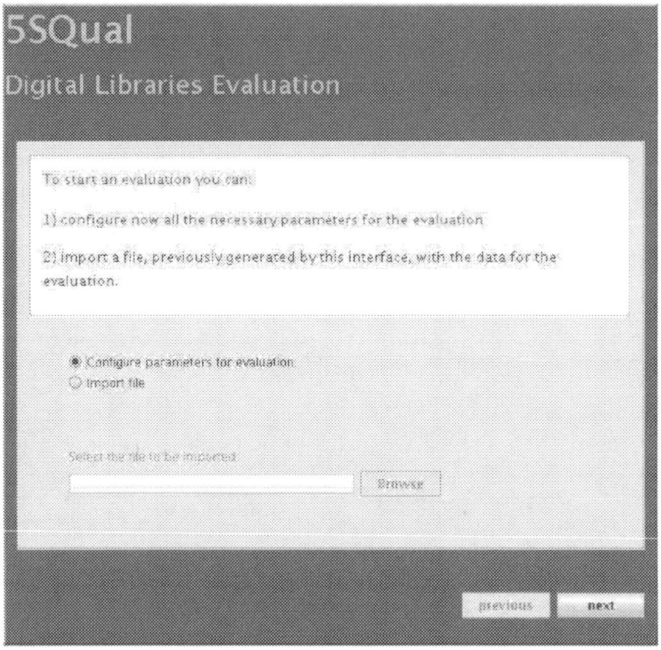

Figure 1.6: 5SQual interface—starting configuration.

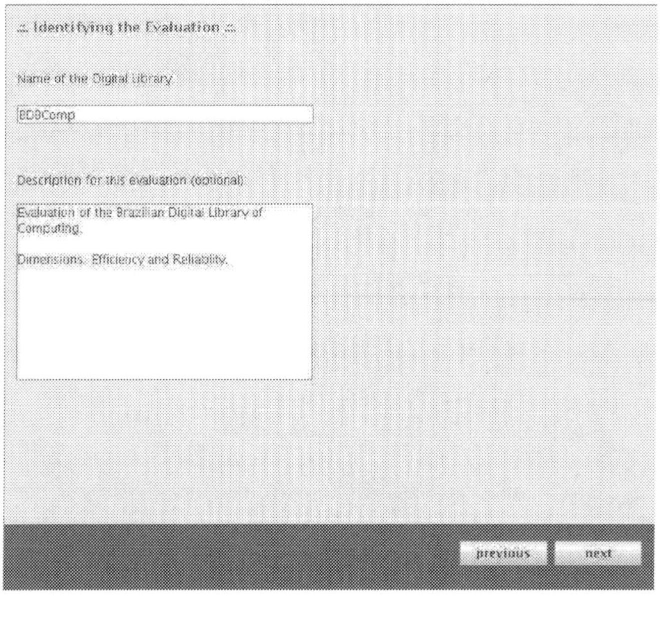

Figure 1.7: 5SQual interface—evaluation identification.

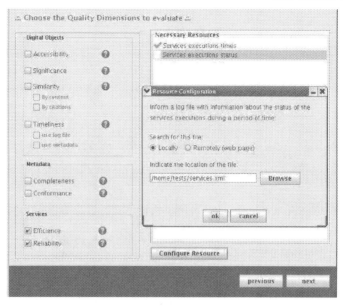

Figure 1.8: 5SQual interface—selection of dimensions and indication of resources.

be used for future evaluations. After this, she chooses whether 5SQual should generate graphics and the final report to show the results of the evaluation, and defines in which directory to save them.

Before calling the configured evaluation, the user can verify a summary of the performed configuration as shown in Figure 1.11. From there, she can choose to go to a previous step and redo some configurations or confirm the current ones. In case of a confirmation, the user can execute the evaluation immediately or run it later. The configuration file is generated in either case.

1.8.2   DL EVALUATIONS USING 5SQUAL

To show the functioning of 5SQual, we have performed a set of evaluations that cover all the dimensions implemented by the tool. For this, we used three different DLs, with different characteristics. We defined the set of dimensions to be evaluated on each DL, according to the availability of the resources required for each dimension to be evaluated. Below, we describe the three DLs and the chosen dimensions for each DL.

- Virginia Tech's Digital Library of Electronic Theses and Dissertations (VT-ETD),[24] is a well-established DL that provides access to full-text documents with different levels of access rights. For this DL, we obtained metadata through the OAI-PMH, therefore allowing to evaluate

[24]http://scholar.lib.vt.edu/theses/

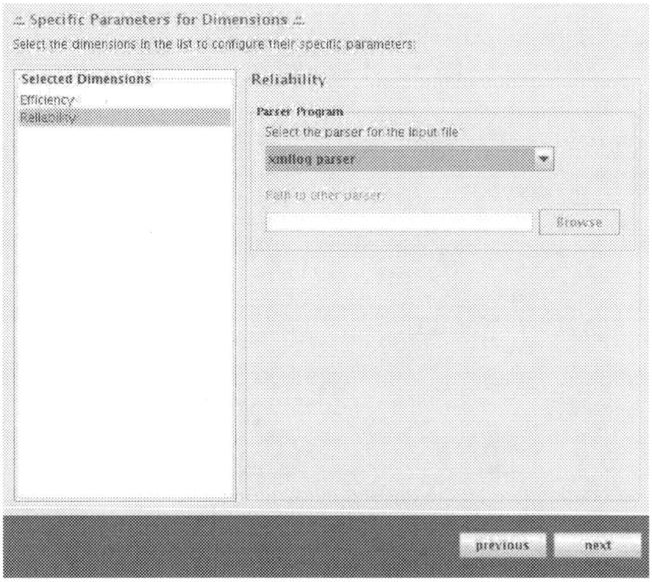

Figure 1.9: 5SQual interface—specification of parameters.

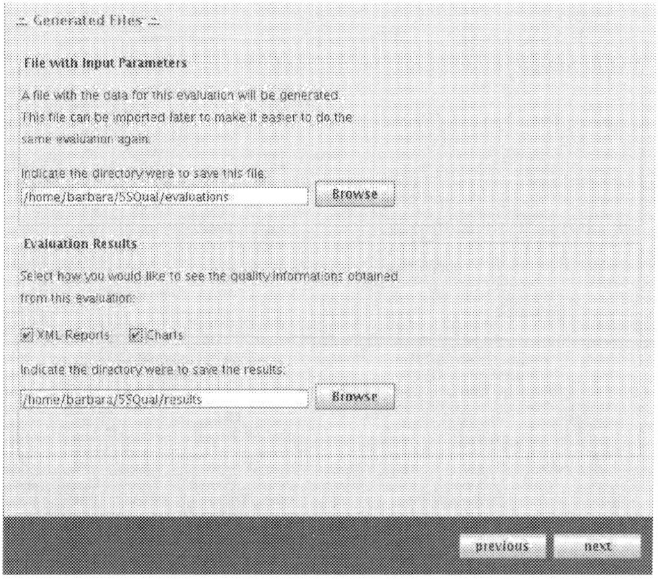

Figure 1.10: 5SQual interface—definition of target for the outputs.

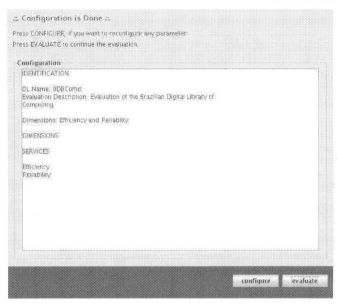

Figure 1.11: 5SQual interface—confirmation of the configuration.

Completeness and Conformance. Since the VT-ETD metadata provides information about access policies and creation date, we also evaluated *Accessibility* and *Timeliness*.

- The Brazilian Digital Library of Computing (BDBComp),[25] see [60], is a DL whose catalog has been built from several distinct sources. In this DL, we had easy access to its log files, allowing us to evaluate the Efficiency and Reliability of its services.

- The ACM 2002 collection (ACM) has 94,818 metadata records along with their internal citation relationships. This collection has been obtained in connection with the CITIDEL project, see [13, 48]. In this collection we evaluated the dimensions based on citation relationships (Similarity by citations), Significance, and Timeliness based on date of the last citation.

Following this, we present the results obtained for each evaluated dimension, including charts and some data extracted from the evaluation reports. The produced reports show the calculated indicators of the evaluated dimensions. The reports cover the evaluation date, the name of the DL, the evaluations of the selected dimensions, and all the numerical indicators chosen in the configuration. For each {dimension, numerical indicator} pair, the reports include: the number of evaluated items, the mean value and the standard deviation considering all the evaluated items, as well as the maximum and minimum values. All the identifiers of the evaluated items are listed in

[25]http://www.lbd.dcc.ufmg.br/bdbcomp/

the reports in decreasing order of the numerical indicator value. This helps to identify outliers or exceptions. An excerpt from a report is shown in Figure 1.12.

```
<AboutEval>
<date>05/01/07</date>                        ⎫  Report Identification
<dlName>DLIB TESTE</dlName>                   ⎬
</AboutEval>                                  ⎭
<Dimension name="Efficiency">◄──────────── Dimension Identification
<indicator name="ResponseTime(seconds)">◄──── Dimension numeric indicator
<numItems>60</numItems> ◄──────────────── Number of evaluated items
<avgValue>1.7</avgValue>                      ⎫
<stdDeviation>2.16</stdDeviation>            ⎬  Summary Results
<maxValue>11.0</maxValue>                     ⎪
<minValue>0.0</minValue>                      ⎭
<evaluations>◄───────────────────────── Results for each evaluated item
<evaluation value="11.0" numOfItems="1">
<itemID>SearchByYear - 04/01/07-18:14:41/04/01/07-18:14:52</itemID>
</evaluation>
<evaluation value="10.0" numOfItems="1">
<itemID>SearchByYear - 04/01/07-18:14:21/04/01/07-18:14:31</itemID>
</evaluation>
   ··· Other evaluation figures
</evaluations>
```

Figure 1.12: 5SQual report excerpt.

VT-ETD Evaluation

From the VT-ETD catalog,[26] we harvested 8,708 metadata records on January 9, 2007 for calculating four dimensions: Accessibility, Completeness, Timeliness, and Conformance.

Accessibility   The VT-ETD metadata includes the *rights* field, with information about the policy for accessing the digital objects from the DL. Objects can be restricted (available only to the VT community), unrestricted (public), or mixed (parts are public and other parts are restricted). For quantitative evaluation, we associated a value of accessibility to each one of these categories— unrestricted: 1, restricted: 0, and mixed: 0.5. To define these values, we considered the view of an actor that does not belong to the VT community.

The chart obtained from the 5SQual evaluation, shown in Figure 1.13, presents the number of objects with restricted, unrestricted, and mixed access. From the corresponding XML report, it is possible to get the identifiers of the documents for each access category.

As we can see, almost 35% of the ETDs had restricted access to those outside of the university environment, which may reveal (largely ungrounded) apprehension, from some of the new graduates, that free availability of the material might cause problems in future attempts to publish the results

---

[26]http://scholar.lib.vt.edu/theses/OAI2/

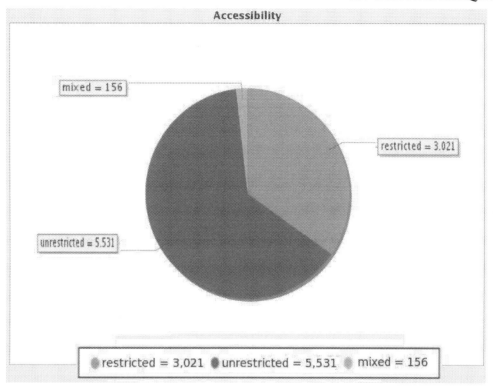

Figure 1.13: VT-ETD—accessibility chart.

of their research as scientific papers or patents. Also, the small number of mixed ETDs (less than 2%) may be due to a lack of knowledge by these graduates about the possibility of releasing only parts of the ETDs, an interesting mechanism that can at the same time protect part of the content while publicizing some of the results.

The results of this evaluation, besides revealing to the administrator the behavior of the users who ingest content in the DL, also may indicate alternatives to modify this behavior in the case it is not the desired one. A strategy to increase the accessibility of this material would be to identify the restricted ETDs (using the evaluation report) and to present to their respective authors, and also to other potential authors, the possibility of releasing only portions of their work through mixed access.

Timeliness The creation time of the digital objects was extracted by 5SQual from the *date* field of the VT ETD metadata records to calculate their timeliness, which in this case was measured in years, given by the difference between the current time and the obtained creation time.

Figure 1.14 presents the chart generated by 5SQual for timeliness. It shows the number of items concentrated under each of the shown timeliness values that were calculated based on the current time (date of this evaluation was January 9, 2007). The y axis shows the number of objects that were created on a specific date, and the x axis determines the date when the objects were inserted in the collection.

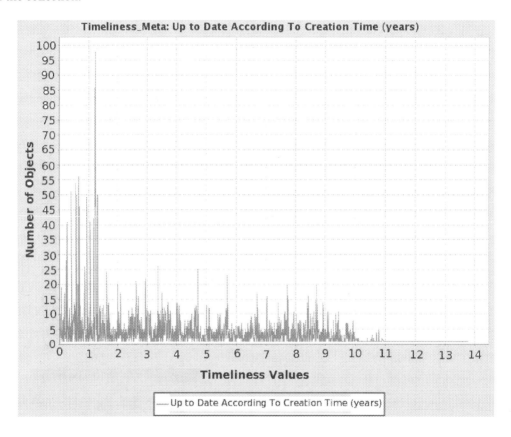

Figure 1.14: VT-ETD—timeliness chart.

From this chart, we can see that objects have been continuously created in this DL over the last 10 years and that many objects (almost 100) were inserted on the same date, approximately 1.3 year ago, when scanning of the backfile was speeding up. We also note that, in the early days of this DL, there was a very stable insertion pattern over the years, which might indicate that the insertion of new objects into the collection was related to some academic events. However, in the last three years this pattern has changed, increasing not only the number of objects per insertion, but also the frequency in which these insertions take place.

From the corresponding XML report, it is possible to find more specific information such as the age of each object, the average object age (4.37 years), and the standard deviation (2.99 years) of the whole collection. In addition, we can see that the oldest object (identified by oai:VTETD:etd-

81197-16953) is 13.76 years old and that the newest one (identified by oai:VTETD:etd-12142006-164331) was created on the date of the evaluation. This reveals that VT-ETD is a DL that keeps its content very timely, what might be due to the fact that the submission of electronic dissertations is mandatory at Virginia Tech.

Completeness   For calculating completeness, we retrieved the VT ETD metadata records which follow the Dublin Core format. This format defines fifteen fields. The Completeness of a metadata record is given by the number of fields present in a record among the fifteen.

The chart in Figure 1.15 shows that there are four distinct completeness values in the catalog. This indicates that there are four groups of records with the same number of fields. The largest group (7,470 records) presents the highest level for completeness in the catalog. The records of this group include 13 of the 15 fields defined by the Dublin Core format, which corresponds to a completeness value near to 0.87. Looking at the other groups, 24 records present completeness equal to 0.67, 1162 have value 0.73, and 52 have the value 0.80. No record is totally complete.

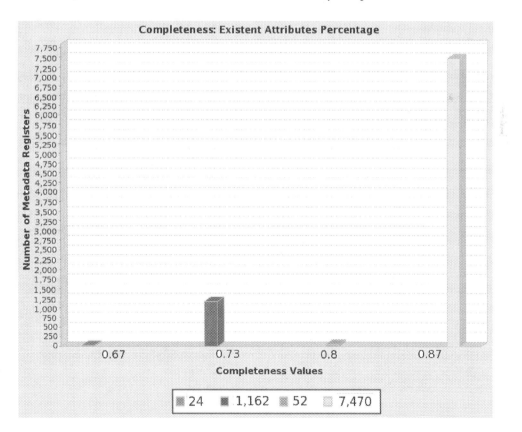

Figure 1.15: VT-ETD—completeness chart.

From the corresponding XML report, we can obtain for this dimension its average value (0.85) and the standard deviation (0.05). The high average and low standard deviation shows that the catalog of this particular DL is quite complete. Furthermore, retrieving the metadata records using their corresponding identifiers in the XML report, it is possible to check which fields are missing. For instance, for the 0.67 group, the one with the lowest level of completeness, we found that the missing fields were relation, coverage, description, contributor, and subject. Analyzing this dimension, the administrator of a DL can have a clear idea of what is missing from its catalog and therefore of the required work for improving it.

Conformance   The Dublin Core format does not place any restriction on the minimum and maximum number of times a field should appear. To evaluate conformance, we have considered a specific set of Dublin Core fields (title, creator, subject, publisher, date, and rights) as mandatory, i.e., we required that they should appear at least once.

The chart in Figure 1.16 shows the VT-ETD conformance evaluation regarding this particular set of restrictions. As we can see, all records exhibit high levels of conformance. The fact that there are just two distinct values for this dimension indicates that either the records are totally in conformance with the imposed restrictions (conformance value equal to 1.0) or that they have just one field that is not in conformance with them (conformance value equal to 0.93). The chart also shows that only 25 records were not totally in conformance with these restrictions.

Analyzing the XML report, we can identify the 25 records in the 0.93 conformance group. When we looked at these records, we find that 24 of them do not have the subject field, and that one record, identified by oai:VTETD:etd-08292003-154546, does not have the title field filled in.

BDBComp Evaluation

Due to easy access to BDBComp log files, we focused evaluation of this DL on two dimensions: efficiency and reliability. These dimensions were evaluated based on the behavior of the search and browse services. Initially, the necessary data to calculate these dimensions would be extracted from the XMLLog file [60] in use by BDBComp, but because of problems during the generation of this file, the data about the request and response times and the status of the executions were lost. Hence, to illustrate these two dimensions, we extracted information from the Apache logs for reliability and simulated some requests for search services (also according to Apache logs) to calculate efficiency. This information would be easily extracted from the XMLLog file since 5SQual already comes with a suitable parser.

Efficiency   To evaluate efficiency, we generated a series of search executions based on the most common queries according to the BDBComp Apache log file. On January 5, 2007, 60 requests were sent to five different BDBComp search services (Search By Author, By Year, By Event, By Title, and By Journal), and for each execution we stored the identifier of the service along with its request and response times, specified in seconds. The generated files followed the 5SQual internal format, which means that an external parser was not required.

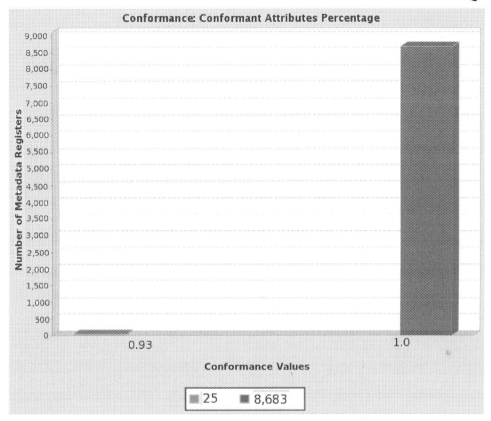

Figure 1.16: VT-ETD—conformance chart.

The chart in Figure 1.17 shows the number of executions for each distinct response time. For instance, we can see that 15 of the 60 executions were processed in less than one second and that the slowest execution lasted 11 seconds.

From the XML report (an excerpt from it is shown in Figure 1.12), we can obtain more specific information about this evaluation. For instance, the slowest service, which took about 11 seconds to produce an answer, was Search by Year. Further investigation revealed the reasons. Due to the structure of the relational database that implements the BDBComp catalog, the SQL query processing for this kind of search yields a response set that is relatively large when compared with the other ones. Since the search processing time varies linearly with the size of the response set, this explains the poor performance of this specific type of search. The range of the desired year period also has an impact on the query processing time, since it determines the relative size of the result set. When we analyzed the results, we noticed that the two slowest queries were the ones of type Search by Year for which the largest year ranges (1900–2000 and 1990–1998) were specified.

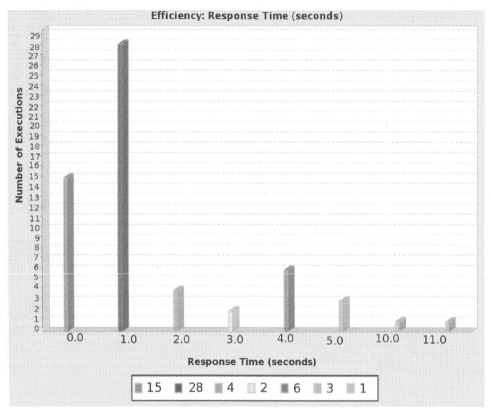

Figure 1.17: BDBComp—efficiency chart.

Reliability   To evaluate reliability, we extracted data from the BDBComp Apache log files, with 5SQual employing an external parser we created. The Apache logs cover the period between April 14, 2005 and January 3, 2007. We analyzed the searching and browsing services. The chart in Figure 1.18 reflects that 634,250 executions were evaluated, where 35,657 (5.6%) ended in a failure.

   The corresponding XML report shows additional information. For instance, it reveals that from the failures only one corresponds to Search By Title and that all the rest of the failures are browsing services. Further investigation revealed that these failures were due to a period of instability of the server, when it went down many times. Additionally, considering the score for a success as 1 and the score for a failure as 0, the average value was 0.94, which means that BDBComp services were quite reliable during the full analyzed period.

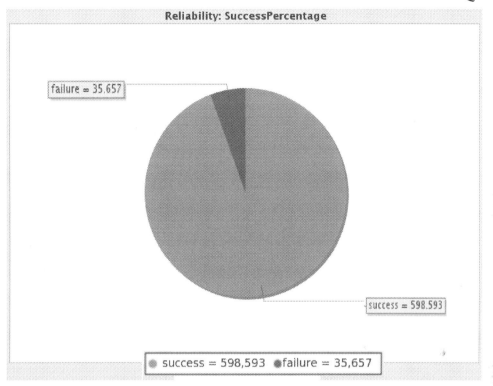

Figure 1.18: BDBComp—reliability chart.

2002 ACM Collection Evaluation

The information about citations among digital objects is an important resource for quality evaluation, making it possible to calculate indicators for three dimensions: similarity, significance, and timeliness. To demonstrate the evaluation of these dimensions, we used the ACM 2002 collection of 94,919 metadata records which include citation information and publication dates for each object.

Significance   We evaluated the significance of a digital object in the ACM collection according to the number of citations it receives from other objects in the collection. For this evaluation, 5SQual generated the chart in Figure 1.19. It shows that the majority of the objects have very few citations within the collection and that there are just a small number of documents with a high significance value.

   The XML report details information about this evaluation, specifying for each object its respective number of citations within the collection. The maximum number of citations to a document is 328 in ACM 2002 (for the document "Computer programming as an art"). There are 51,925 objects without citations. The average number of citations an object receives is 2.35 (this number refers

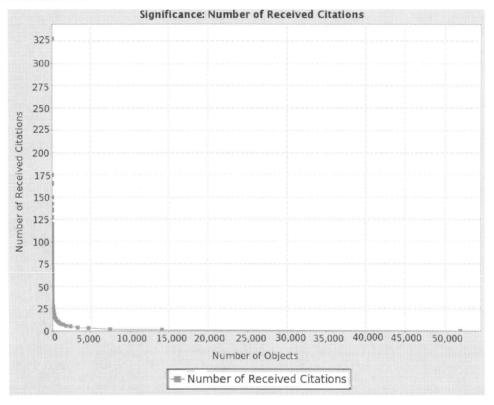

Figure 1.19: ACM—significance chart.

just to citations of papers that are in the ACM collection). The high standard deviation value (6.16) shows that the number of citations has high variability.

Similarity By Citations   To illustrate similarity by citations, we have chosen to compare, against the whole collection, two digital objects: the one with the most out-citations (i.e., the references that appear in a document) and the one with the most in-citations (i.e., the citations a document receives). We used two numeric indicators for these comparisons: co-citation [107], considering the document with more in-citations as the reference one, and bibliographic coupling [55] to compare the document with more out-citations against the others. Two documents are co-cited if a third one has citations to both of them (i.e., if they have in-citations in common). The more in-citations in common the more related or similar they are. Bibliographic coupling looks for common out-citations in the two objects being compared.

Bar charts for these evaluations are given in Figures 1.20 and 1.21. They show the number of objects with similarity to the reference documents inside certain intervals. The width of the intervals was obtained by dividing the size of the whole interval (given by the difference between the maximum and the minimum similarity value) by the number of bars. From this we see that the similarity values for co-citation are roughly an order of magnitude smaller than those for bibliographic coupling. This is unsurprising, since co-citations are relatively rare, and the bibliographic coupling values in a medium-sized collection of works in a focused domain are likely to be significantly higher. Thus, references in the documents (out-citations) contribute more to similarity than the citations they receive (in-citations). Nevertheless, both evaluations indicate similar behavior in that the majority of the objects are concentrated in the first interval, which covers the smallest similarity values.

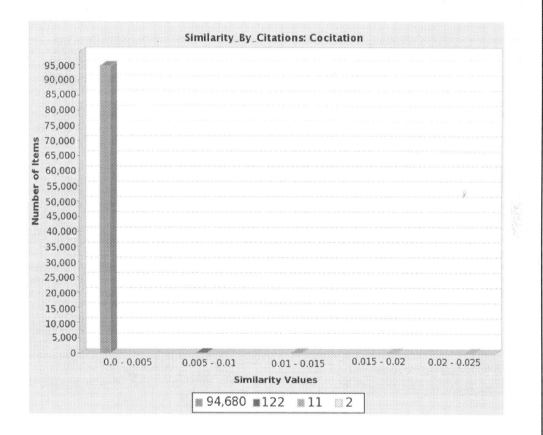

Figure 1.20: ACM—similarity chart—co-citation.

5SQual also tells us that in the ACM 2002 collection there are more digital objects without in-citations (51,925) than without out-citations (46,331). These results are consistent with [16], where it was shown that for DLs containing scientific papers, measures based on bibliographic coupling are more appropriate for similarity detection.

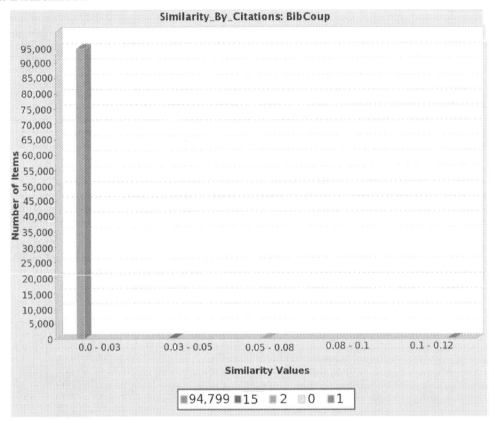

Figure 1.21: ACM—similarity chart—bibliographic coupling.

Timeliness   For the ACM 2002 collection, we used timeliness regarding the last date a specific digital object was cited, considering only the internal citations within the collection. For this collection, this date marks the end of the period of influence of the information contained in the object.

Our evaluation was performed on January 14, 2007. Hence, as expected, since the analyzed collection is from 2002, Figure 1.22 shows that the objects more recently cited received citations four or more years earlier. The figure also shows that many objects received citations between 4.5 and 7 years ago and that there are objects that were not cited for more than 55 years.

In the report, it is possible to identify each individual object and the timeliness value associated with it.

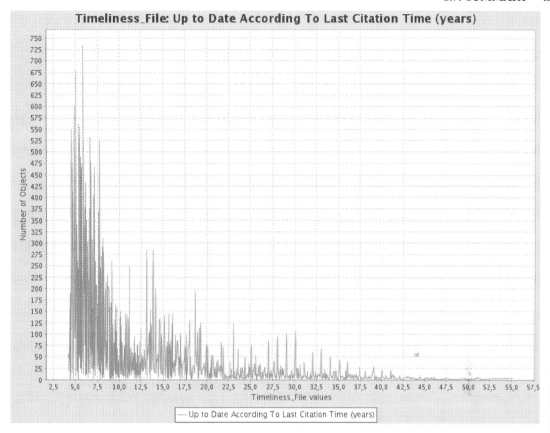

Figure 1.22: ACM—timeliness chart.

1.9 SUMMARY

We proposed candidate dimensions of quality for some of the most important DL concepts and factors affecting the measurement of the corresponding quality dimensions within the 5S framework. Based on a formal quality model for digital libraries, we developed 5SQual. This tool helps to manage and maintain DLs through automatic and recurrent evaluations that can help administrators to diagnose problems and suggest possible improvements to the system and its data, as well as demonstrate their evolution over time.

1.10 EXERCISES AND PROJECTS

1. What are some of the worst problems you have observed in working with digital libraries? What evaluation approach(es) might be used to identify occurrences of such problems?

2. What kind of evaluation methods are used by commercial search engines? Why?

3. What other types of evaluation might apply to digital objects, and how might they be assessed? Please consider this with regard to each of the following types of DLs: bibliographic/metadata-only, full-text, hypertext, hypermedia (considering separately or together systems handling representations such as images, videos, music, 3D-graphics, software programs, and CAD/CAM).

4. What other types of evaluation might apply to metadata information in DLs? How can the values in metadata fields be checked/validated, separately or in combination?

5. Assume you have a large DL and want to improve the quality of the content using machine learning. How might you do this?

6. Assume you manage a DL that gets data from a number of sources, and find that some sources have lower quality than other sources. What types of policies might you establish so that quality improves? How could you use evaluation methods to help you enforce those policies?

7. Assume you have evaluated services in your DL and found some performance problems, but cannot pinpoint the causes of the problems. How might you extend the logging system in your DL, so you can better identify and solve problems?

8. Could 5SQual be applied to a DL that you work with? What would be required for that to occur?

9. What are some extensions to 5SQual that you consider important relative to your interests in DLs? How might those extensions be implemented?

10. Which of the ideas covered in this chapter might apply to evaluating parts of the WWW? How might you undertake such evaluations? What improvements do you expect might result?

11. Sometimes it is useful to carry out evaluations on a regular basis. If that were done with a DL familiar to you, what might be learned? What are some of the changes that might be observed? What might those changes indicate?

CHAPTER 2

Integration

Abstract: In this chapter, we formalize and solve the key problem of digital library (DL) integration, explained in the context of related work. An integrated Archaeological DL, ETANA-DL, is used as a case study to justify and evaluate our integration approach. Accordingly, we also demonstrate how to develop domain specific DLs according to the 5S (Streams, Structures, Spaces, Scenarios, and Societies) framework.

Our discussion extends the brief related discussions in the first book of this series. There, in Appendix C, we first formalize the DL integration problem and then propose an overall approach based on the 5S framework. That provides a systematic and functional method to design and implement DL exploring services. More specifically, we develop a minimal metamodel for archaeological DLs within the 5S theory. Further, in Appendix D, we describe the 5SSuite tool set to cover the process of union DL generation, including requirements gathering, conceptual modeling, rapid prototyping, and code generation. 5SSuite consists of 5SGraph, 5SGen, and SchemaMapper, each of which plays an important role in DL integration.

2.1   INTRODUCTION

2.1.1   THE DIGITAL LIBRARY INTEGRATION PROBLEM

DLs are transforming research, scholarship, and education at all levels. One of the intriguing aspects of DL research is that challenges exist at both the fundamental technology level and at the large-scale integration level. Over two decades of government and private funding of DL research projects has led to important results at the fundamental technology level. The successes in large-scale integration are arguably less evident. Even the notion of "DL integration" is ambiguous in the sense that different approaches and proposed solutions exist. Work on DL integration focuses to an extent on three issues [46]:

1. distribution: geographical spread;

2. heterogeneity: difference at both the technical level (e.g., hardware platform, operating system, programming language, etc.) and conceptual level (e.g., different understanding and modeling of the same real-world entities); and

3. autonomy: the extent to which the components are self-sufficient, as opposed to being delegated a role only as components in a larger system.

By DL integration, we mean hiding distribution and heterogeneity, while at the same time enabling and making visible component autonomy (at least to some degree).

Many DLs belonging to different organizations were developed independently without plans to provide open and easily automated access to their data and functionality. The inability to seamlessly and transparently access knowledge across DLs is a major impediment to knowledge sharing. The goal of DL integration then is to utilize various autonomous DLs in concert to provide knowledge hidden in such island-DLs. The needs for DL integration are well known, and better known than the solutions [62].

Challenges to DL integration are a direct result of DL characteristics. DLs are complex information systems due to their inherently interdisciplinary nature, both with regard to application domains and technologies involved in building the systems. Concerning the latter, DL system implementations integrate findings from disciplines such as hypertext, information retrieval, multimedia services, database management, and human-computer interaction [29]. Hence, an integrative theory for DL is needed. [36] summarizes key early work on the 5S (Streams, Structures, Spaces, Scenarios, and Societies) framework and related efforts to construct such an integrative theory for DLs. The 5S framework allows us to define digital libraries rigorously and usefully. Streams are sequences of arbitrary items used to describe both static and dynamic (e.g., video) content. Structures can be viewed as labeled directed graphs, which impose organization. Spaces are sets with operations that obey certain constraints. Scenarios consist of sequences of events or actions that modify states of a computation in order to accomplish a functional requirement. Societies are sets of entities and activities, and the relationships among them. Together these abstractions provide a formal foundation to define, relate, and unify concepts—among others, of digital objects, metadata, collections, and services—required to formalize and elucidate "digital libraries" [35].

DL integration can be done at different levels, e.g., information level and service level. Integrated information makes distributed collections of heterogeneous resources appear to be a single union collection. Integrated services provide users more comprehensive usage of DL resources through more coherent and easier to use interfaces that hide syntax and semantic differences in the DLs to be integrated.

Developing an infrastructure to address all perspectives of the DL integration problem is an ambitious task. While many efforts have looked into the DL integration problem, most developed their own approaches in an ad hoc and piecemeal fashion. The DL integration problem formalization and an overall approach based on the 5S framework are introduced in the first book of this series. Below, we extend that discussion and apply our framework to integrate domain specific (archaeological) DLs, illustrating our approach with regard to key sub-problems (e.g, semantic interoperability) of DL integration.

2.1.2 HYPOTHESIS AND RESEARCH QUESTIONS

We claim that the 5S framework provides effective solutions to DL integration. This hypothesis leads to the following research questions.

1. Can we formally define the DL integration problem, using the 5S framework?

2. Can the 5S framework guide integration of domain/discipline focused DLs (e.g., integrate systems for diverse archaeological sites into a union archaeological DL)? If yes, how? Specifically:

   • How can we formally model such domain specific DLs in the 5S framework?

   • How can we integrate DL models into a union DL model?

   • How can we use the union DL model to help design and implement high quality integrated DLs?

3. Can we assess an integrated DL based on a set of indicators and metrics? What are those? How well does the integration work in practice?

2.2   RELATED WORK

The issues or challenges to be solved for achieving integration are referred to and categorized differently in the relevant literature. For example, considering education, Virkus et al. [118] have given an extensive overview of the issues and challenges of the integration of digital libraries and virtual learning environments (VLEs). Further, considering heterogeneous distributed systems, interoperability is a key issue when integrating heterogeneous DLs [1, 75, 86]. Alternatively, considering global concerns, on May 16-17, 2011, the Berkman Center together with Open Knowledge Commons and the Institute for Information Law at the University of Amsterdam convened a group of technical and legal experts from public and research libraries and government agencies in the U.S. and Europe for a workshop focused on key questions regarding global interoperability in DLs.

Interoperability is a broad problem with many dimensions [74, 75] and has been the subject of many initiatives. Typically, it has been investigated within a specific scope, such as within a particular community (e.g., libraries, commercial entities, and scientific communities), within a particular type of information (e.g., electronic records, technical reports, and software), or within a particular information technology area (e.g., relational databases, digital imaging, and information visualization) [78]. Various aspects of DL interoperability are depicted in Fig. 2.1, a concept map for the problem.

Research on interoperability in DL architectures addresses the challenges of creating a general framework for information access and integration across many of the above domains. A common goal of these efforts is to enable different communities, with different types of information and technologies, to achieve a general level of information sharing and, through the process of aggregation and computation, to create new and more powerful types of information.

There are many approaches to achieving interoperability. Paepcke et al. [75] have categorized many of the prevalent approaches and have provided an informative discussion of the challenges inherent in creating interoperable DLs of global scope. Some of the common approaches have included: (1) standardization (e.g., schema definition, data model, and protocol), (2) distributed object request

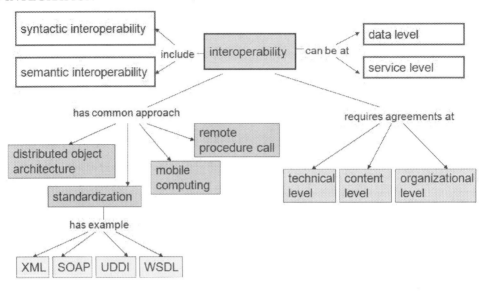

Figure 2.1: Various aspects of interoperability in DLs [103].

architectures (e.g., CORBA), (3) remote procedure calls, (4) mediation (e.g., gateways, wrappers), and (5) mobile computing (e.g., with Java applets). Considering the first of these approaches, for example, Suleman [109] presented some of the key principles and practices of DL interoperability. He described standardization of protocols—such as HTTP, XML and web services—and how they have been combined in the Open Archives Initiative [73]. The Open Archives Initiative developed the Protocol for Metadata Harvesting in response to a need for a low barrier to interoperability. The protocol allows for the exchange of a stream of XML-encoded records between two machines operating in client-server mode.

To achieve DL interoperability requires agreement to cooperate at three levels: technical, content, and organizational [5]. Technical agreements cover formats, protocols, security systems, etc., so that messages can be exchanged. Content agreements cover the data and metadata, and include semantic agreements on the interpretation of the information. Organizational agreements cover the ground rules for access, preservation of collections and services, payments, authentication, etc.

There are two different types of interoperability for DL integration [76]: syntactic interoperability and semantic interoperability. Syntactic interoperability is the application-level interoperability that allows multiple software components to cooperate even though their implementation languages, interfaces, and execution platforms are different. Semantic interoperability is the knowledge-level interoperability that allows DLs to be integrated, with the ability to bridge semantic conflicts arising from differences in implicit meanings, perspectives, and assumptions, thus creating a semantically compatible information environment based on agreed-upon concepts (among various DLs). Standards such as XML and web services based on SOAP (Simple Object Access Protocol), UDDI (Universal Description Discovery and Integration), and WSDL (Web Service Description Language) can resolve many application-level interoperability problems [76]. However, establishing semantic interoperability among heterogeneous information sources from various DLs continues to be a critical issue. The NSF Post Digital Libraries Futures Workshop [63] identified it as being of primary importance in digital library research. DELOS WP5 [77] reported many issues relating to semantic interoperability in DLs. Next, we present related work concerning semantic interoperability in DLs.

2.2.1   SEMANTIC INTEROPERABILITY IN DIGITAL LIBRARIES

Semantic interoperability in DLs means the capability of different information systems to communicate information consistent with the intended meaning [77]. Information integration is only one possible result of a successful communication. Since the emergence of different human languages, communication can be achieved in two ways: (1) force everyone to learn and use the same language; (2) find translators who know how to interpret sufficiently the information of one participant for another. The first approach is proactive standardization, while the second one is reactive interpretation. This choice applies to all levels and functions of semantic interoperability and is a major distinctive criterion of various methods. [58] provides a solid grounding in the principles, research, design, architecture, and implementation of semantic digital libraries and their uses. [79] collects selected high-quality chapters by researchers from both academia and industry about semantic interoperability and related issues. Related work concerning DL semantic interoperability is presented as a concept map in Fig. 2.2.

Standardization

One of the traditional approaches to interoperability is for all participants to agree to use the same standards, such as metadata standards and transaction protocols. Standardization has the following advantages.

- Information can be immediately transferred and integrated without transformation and alteration.

- Information can be kept in a single form.

- Information can be enforced to be functionally complete for an envisaged integrated service.

The disadvantages are the following.

- Information needs adaptation to the standard. The adaptation may require interpretation (manual or automatic) and may result in information loss.

- The effort of producing a standard may be very high.

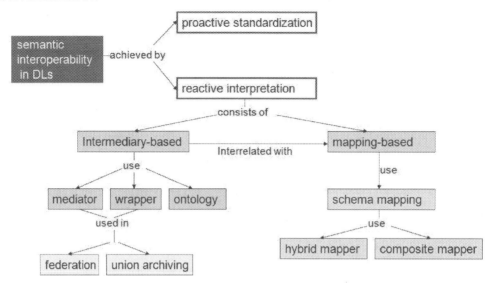

Figure 2.2: A concept map for related work on semantic interoperability in DLs [103].

- A standard has to foresee all future use. Introducing a new element may be time consuming and may cause upwards-compatibility problems.

- A standard is designed to suit its domain. It may not be optimal for all applications.

A standard is elegant and efficient for specific applications. It is appropriate for problems with a low degree of necessary diversity and with high long-term stability. Examples of metadata standards are DC (Dublin Core), Dublin Core with DC-Ed extensions, FGDC (Content Standard for Digital Geospatial Metadata), IEEE LOM (Learning Objects Metadata), and METS (Metadata Encoding and Transmission Standard). DC can be considered as a minimal standard, while METS provides a flexible mechanism for encoding descriptive, administrative, and structural metadata for a digital library object, and for expressing the complex relationships between these various forms of metadata. METS therefore can provide a useful standard for the exchange of digital library objects between repositories. In addition, METS provides the ability to associate a digital object with behaviors or services.

Interpretation
Examples of interpretation in a DL are mapping of one metadata framework to another (metadata crosswalk) and correlation of concepts defined in knowledge organization systems (KOS). Interpretation has the following advantages.

- Information to be integrated, in particular legacy data, needs no adaptation. Only application relevant parts need interpretation.

- Interpretation can be optimized for multiple functions and interpreters can easily be adapted to changes.

The disadvantages are:

- The manual effort of producing the knowledge base (e.g., correlation tables for terminologies) for an interpreter can be very high, though automatic generation is feasible.

- Interpretation of information may result in information loss.

- The number of interpreters needed increases drastically if the number of formats in use increases. In such situations, interpretation may need to go through a common switching language, which reduces the number of interpreters needed, but increases the loss of precision. Effectively, such a switching language is another standard.

Interpreters are effective in environments with a high degree of necessary diversity and low long-term stability.

As shown in the concept map about related work concerning DL semantic interoperability in Fig. 2.2, two approaches to interoperability through interpretation are interrelated. They are the intermediary-based approach and the mapping-based approach. The intermediary-based approach depends on the use of intermediary mechanisms such as mediators, wrappers, and ontologies to achieve interoperability. The mapping-based approach attempts to construct mappings between semantically related information sources. It is usually accomplished by constructing a global schema and by establishing mappings between the global schema and the local schemas. Approaches based on intermediaries may rely on mapping knowledge, domain-specific knowledge, or rules established by mapping-based approaches.

1. Interoperability through interpretation by intermediary mechanisms

1.1. Wrappers and mediators.

Wrappers and mediators provide information manipulation services over a reconciled view of heterogeneous data. Wrappers encapsulate details of each information source, allowing data access under a homogeneous data representation and manipulation style (common data model or standardized schema). Mediators offer an integrated view of the information sets of several information sources associated with corresponding wrappers or other mediators. Some systems adopt multiple levels of mediators in order to modularize the information transformation and integration along successive levels of abstraction.

Two wrappers and one mediator providing integrated access to two different information sources are shown in Fig. 2.3. The mediator brokers the requests from the application into requests to the wrappers of the corresponding information sources involved. On receiving the replies from the source wrappers, the mediator composes the results to return an integrated result to the application. Information transformation and mapping specifications may be used to drive the functioning of mediators and wrappers. Wrapper generators and data mapping specification languages enable the specification of data integration in a more intelligible manner than using conventional programming languages to hard code wrappers and mediators.

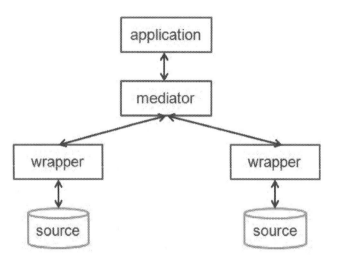

Figure 2.3: Wrappers and mediators [103].

1.2. Ontology

One of the well-accepted mechanisms for achieving semantic interoperability is the utilization of ontologies[1] [43]. Structure knowledge embedded in ontologies supports information retrieval and interoperability. Ontologies also help the investigation of correspondences between elements of heterogeneous data sources.[2] Related research proposes the development of information systems components by translating ontologies into object-oriented hierarchies for implementation, giving rise to the concept of ontology-driven information systems.

There is no universal agreement with respect to the form of a machine-processable ontology. A simple hierarchy specifying classes and their subsumption relationships (e.g., a taxonomy) is a simple type of ontology. Likewise, a relational database schema that includes a specification of relationships and integrity constraints, also can be considered as an ontology.

---

[1]We introduce ontologies now with respect to interoperability, but cover them in more detail in a focused chapter in the next book of this DL series.
[2]This is one of the key objectives of the Ensemble project, which is working to use an ontology for computing to connect topically related educational resources coming from the diverse communities interested in computing. [27]

Several languages and formalisms have been proposed to express knowledge in ontologies. OWL (Web Ontology Language) [19] is one of the most prominent ontology languages for the Semantic Web. It was extended from RDF [90].

The development of ontologies is a labor intensive and error-prone task if it is done manually. Ontology engineering tools can automate parts of this task and hide the idiosyncrasies of the ontology specification languages and formalisms. Through visual interfaces, those tools help knowledge acquisition, remote access to knowledge repositories, syntax checking, and quality validation.

1.3. Federation

Within the intermediary-based approach there are two possible architectures to deal with the problem of integration, namely, federation and union archiving (see Fig. 2.2). Federation refers to the case where the DL sends search criteria to multiple remote repositories and the results are gathered, combined, and presented to the user [37, 65, 82]. Federation is a more expensive mode of operation in terms of network and search system constraints since each repository has to support a complex search language and fast real-time response to queries.

In recent years, major Web search engines have extended their services to include search on specialized subcollections or verticals focused on specific domains (e.g., news, travel, and local search) or media types (e.g., images and video). Content from specialized corpora or verticals can be integrated into Web search results when a user issues a query. In the research community, this is referred to as federated search.

Federated search aggregates heterogeneous types of results from multiple vertical search engines, and composes a single search engine result page (SERP). The search engine aggregates the results and produces one ranked list. It improves search when the user has vertical intent but may not be aware of vertical search.

Vertical results are presented in small boxes refered to as the direct display (DD) and are frequently shown at specific slots (positions). Fig. 2.4 gives an example of a SERP rendered by Yahoo! search. In response to a query name 'pizza', a local DD is displayed above the top Web result and an image DD is shown in the middle of the page (below the fourth Web result). A searcher may either click on a displayed link to local content or skip the display by not clicking on that link.

Federated search consists of two phases, vertical selection and SERP composition. Vertical selection determines which verticals should be triggered, while SERP composition concerns where the content from the verticals is placed (slotted) on the SERP. Diaz et al. [20] addressed the vertical selection problem of predicting relevant verticals (if any) for queries sent to the search engine's main Web search page. They sought to estimate the click-through rate of the vertical item direct display by learning a model based on three sources of evidence: (1) the query string, from which features are derived independently of external resources, (2) logs of queries previously issued directly to the vertical, and (3) corpora representative of vertical content. Kumar et al. [81] present a machine-learning framework for SERP composition in the presence of multiple relevant verticals.

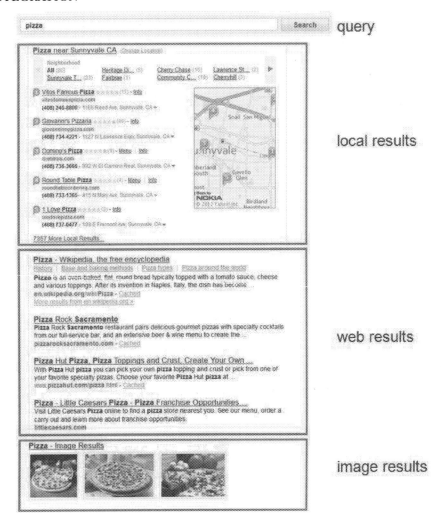

query

local results

web results

image results

Figure 2.4: The Yahoo! SERP showing vertical search results at different slots.

They viewed SERP composition as a ranking problem. Given the different types of verticals, the goal is to construct the SERP with the most relevant information.

1.4. Union archiving and related projects

Union archiving is based on a mechanism to gather or harvest data from the sources and to load them into a centralized data store. The difficulty of creating large federations that lead to quality results and fast response time is the motivation for work on union archiving. The underlying concept is that the participants agree to take small efforts that enable some basic shared services.

As for union archiving, there are several paradigms for harvesting data from heterogeneous sites, such as Harvest [11], OAI (Open Archives Initiative) [73], and SRU (Search/Retrieve URL Service) [111]. The underlying concept of Harvest is to divide the principal functions of a centralized search system into separate subsystems consisting of gatherers and brokers. Gatherers collect indexing information from DL collections, while brokers build a combined index of information about many collections. Harvest defines formats and protocols for communication among gatherers and brokers. OAI is a multi-institutional project to address interoperability of DLs. It provides a simple but extensible metadata harvesting protocol, OAI-PMH (the Open Archives Initiative Protocol for Metadata Harvesting), to support the streaming of metadata from one repository to another. It emphasizes the distinction between data providers and service providers. The former administer systems that support the OAI-PMH as a means of exposing metadata. The latter use metadata harvested via the OAI-PMH as a basis for building value-added services [110]. SRU and OAI-PMH are complementary protocols. Both have a goal to harvest metadata from remote sites, but each provides functionality that the other does not. They differ the most when it comes to retrieval. SRU provides a much more granular approach, at the expense of requiring support for a complex CQL (Common Query Language).

2. Interoperability through interpretation by mapping-based approach

While many research projects have developed semantic mediators and wrappers to address interoperability, few have tackled the problem of (partially) automating production of these mediators and wrappers, which contain specific domain knowledge, such as mappings between source schema and the integrated schema [21]. Schema mapping is typically performed manually, perhaps supported by a graphical user interface, such as Microsoft BizTalk Schema Mapper (`http://www.microsoft.com/biztalk/`) and Altova Mapforce (`http://www.altova.com/mapforce.html`). Manual schema mapping is a tedious, time-consuming, error-prone, and expensive process. This has spurred numerous solutions to automate the mapping process.

While fully automating the mapping process to automatically generate wrappers is generally not feasible, it is possible to implement techniques that reduce the amount of human interaction. Researchers have investigated how schema mappings can be illustrated, refined, or derived using data examples, where a data example is a pair consisting of a source instance and a target instance. Alexe et al. [2] used data examples to illustrate and refine schema mappings, while [3, 41] used data examples to derive schema mappings. In particular, [41] derives a schema mapping from a single data example using a cost model that takes into account several different parameters, including the size of the syntactic description of the schema mapping. In general, given a set of data examples, there may exist several pairwise, logically inequivalent schema mappings that "fit" the given data examples. In [3], an algorithm was designed that, given a finite set of data examples, decides whether or not there exists a GLAV schema mapping (i.e., a schema mapping specified by Global-and-

Local-As-View constraints) that "fits" these data examples. If such a fitting GLAV schema mapping exists, then the algorithm returns the "most general" among such schema mappings. Similar results are obtained in [3] for the case of Global-As-View (GAV) schema mappings.

Cate et al. [115] cast the problem of obtaining algorithmically a schema mapping from data examples as a learning problem and then embark on a systematic investigation of this problem using concepts and methods of computational learning theory. They leveraged the rich body of work on learning theory in order to develop a framework for exploring the power and the limitations of the various algorithmic methods for obtaining schema mappings from data examples.

An implementation of a mapper may involve multiple mapping algorithms, wherein each algorithm computes a mapping based on a single criterion. A hybrid mapper uses multiple mapping criteria, while a composite mapper combines multiple mapping results produced by different mapping algorithms, including hybrid mappers [85]. The ability of composite mappers to combine different mappers is more flexible than that of hybrid mappers. A hybrid mapper typically uses a hard-wired combination of particular mapping techniques that are executed simultaneously or in a fixed order. However, a composite mapper allows selection from a repository of modular mappers, and has the ability to extend the system when additional mappers are needed.

2.2.2   INTEGRATED SERVICES

There are some related works on integrating services in DLs. Some integrate searching and browsing while others integrate searching and browsing with other services. For example, CODER [24], a retrieval and hypertext system using SGML and a lexicon developed in the 1980s, was used as a testbed for the study of artificial intelligence concepts in the field of information retrieval; MARIAN [25], an indexing, search, and retrieval system optimized for digital libraries, was developed in the 1990s; ODL [108], a system built as networks of extended open archives, was developed in 2001.

A synergy between searching and browsing is required to support users' information-seeking goals [9, 10, 33, 34, 67]. Text mining and visualization techniques provide DLs additional powerful exploring services, with possible beneficial effects on searching and browsing. Thus, Stepping Stones & Pathway (SSP) integrates visualization, clustering, and Bayesian inference to support exploration and the resolution of complex information needs that can be met by sets of related documents [18, 30]. CitiViz, a visual interface to CITIDEL, combines searching, browsing, clustering, and information visualization [53].

2.3   CASE STUDY: AN ETANA-DL EXPERIENCE

2.3.1   MODELING OF DOMAIN SPECIFIC DIGITAL LIBRARIES WITH THE 5S FRAMEWORK

Requirements gathering and conceptual modeling are essential for the customization of DLs, to help attend the needs of target communities. In this section, we show how to apply the 5S (Streams, Structures, Spaces, Scenarios, and Societies) formal framework to support both tasks. The intuitive nature of the framework allows for easy and systematic requirements analysis, while its formal nature ensures the precision and correctness required for semi-automatic DL generation. Further, we show how 5S can help us define a domain-specific DL metamodel in the field of archaeology. An archaeological DL case study (from the ETANA project) then yields informal and formal descriptions of two DL models (instances of the metamodel). Finally, we illustrate the use of the 5SGraph tool to specify archaeological DLs.

This section shows how 5S can be used to analyze the requirements of domain-specific DLs. More specifically, it informally describes the archaeological domain, and therefore archaeological DLs (ArchDLs), in the light of the 5S framework. Some work presented in this section is derived from part of the requirements analysis for ETANA-DL, i.e., email interviews with five prestigious archaeologists and face-to-face workplace interviews with eleven archaeologists (including three of the five interviewed by email) conducted by the original PI of the ETANA-DL project, along with the Head of Digital Library Initiatives at Case Western University Reserve University.

1. Societies

Societies can be groups of humans as well as hardware and software components. Examples of human societies in ArchDLs include archaeologists (in academic institutes, fieldwork settings, excavation units, or local / national government bodies), the general public (e.g., educators, learners), and those who lived in historic and prehistoric societies. There also are societies of project directors, field staff (responsible for the work of excavation), technical staff (e.g., photographers, technical illustrators, and their assistants), and camp staff (including camp managers, registrars, and tool stewards). Since archaeology is a multi-disciplinary subject, drawing on a wide range of skills and specialties, from the arts and humanities to the biological and physical sciences, societies of specialists (e.g., in geology, anthropology, lithics, ceramics, faunal and floral remains, remote sensing) are involved in ArchDLs. Societies follow certain rules and their members play particular roles. Members of societies have activities and relationships (e.g., specialists serve to assist and advise the varying field and laboratory staffs regarding field problems and other matters related to their special skills and interests). Because archaeologists in diverse countries follow different laws and customs, a number of ethical and freedom-related issues arise in connection with ArchDLs. Examples include: Who owns the finds? Where should they be preserved? What nationality and ethnicity do they represent? Who has publication rights?

To address these issues, and to support the variety of needs of interested societies, DL designers have planned for numerous scenarios.

2. Scenarios

A scenario is often defined as a description of interactions between a human user and a computerized system. Scenarios also can describe interactions among software modules (as in [36]) or among humans. Further, describing scientific processes (hypothesizing, observing, recording, testing, analyzing, and drawing conclusions—used during any archaeological study) as scenarios can help with comprehending specific ArchDL phenomena, and with requirements elicitation and specification generation.

Digital recording as an archaeological process to facilitate information gathering occurs in two stages, the planning stage and the excavation stage. Remote sensing, fieldwalking, field surveys, building surveys, consulting historical and other documentary sources, and managing the sites and monuments (and related records) maintained by local and national government bodies may be involved in the planning stage. During excavation, detailed information is recorded, including for each layer of soil, and for features such as pole holes, pits, and ditches. Data about each artifact is recorded together with information about its exact find location. Numerous environmental and other samples are taken for laboratory analysis, and the location and purpose of each is carefully recorded. Large numbers of photographs are taken, both general views of the progress of excavation and detailed shots showing the contexts of finds. Since excavation is a destructive process, this makes it imperative that the recording methods are both accurate and reliable. Unlike many other applications of information systems, it simply is not possible to go back and re-check at a later date [94]. Large quantities of archaeological data generated during the above-mentioned two stages can be harvested by ArchDLs, and then organized and stored to be available to researchers outside a project (site), without substantial delay. After excavation, information stored in ArchDLs is analyzed and helps archaeologists to test hypotheses. For example, if archaeologists retrieve records of corn artifacts from an ArchDL, they might hypothesize that the former residents were farmers, and test their hypothesis with soil sample data using statistical analysis tools provided by the ArchDL. This hypothesis is a scenario involving archaeologists, the historical community (farmers), and finds (corn samples). Other hypotheses are scenarios describing relationships among historical communities. For example, if there are large collections of jars of the same style found in two nearby sites, archaeologists might hypothesize that people in these two sites (cities) used the jars to carry things in commercial trade. Thus, primary archaeological data, managed with powerful tools in ArchDLs, help archaeologists find physical relationships between excavation contexts, develop a structural history of a site, and extend the understanding of past material cultures and environments in the area. Data generated from the sites' interpretation then provide a basis for future work including publication, museum displays, and, in due course, input into future project planning.

Besides supporting archaeologists in their work as described above, ArchDLs provide services for the general public. A student interested in a Near Eastern site can access all the archaeological information about it by browsing or using complex retrieval criteria that take into account both intrinsic attributes of items and their extrinsic spatial and temporal interrelationships. Further, she can view the information organized in a spatial hierarchy/map that facilitates navigation among archaeological items at various spatial scales. She can click on items to show details; to display photographs, maps, diagrams, or textual documents; or to jump (link) to other items.

3. Spaces

One important spatial aspect of ArchDLs is the geographic distribution of found artifacts, which are located in a 4D spatial continua, the fourth dimension being the temporal (as inferred by the archaeologists). Metric or vector spaces are used to support retrieval operations, calculate distances, and constrain searches spatially. Other space-related aspects deal with user interfaces or with 3D models of the past.

4. Structures

Structures represent the ways the highly variable information related to archaeology is organized. Archaeological information has spatial, temporal, and topical aspects. Examples include site organizations, timelines, and taxonomies of specific unearthed artifacts like bones and seeds. The structures of sites present, simply and consistently, the basic spatial containment relationship at every level of detail, from the broadest region of archaeological interest to the smallest aspect of an individual find. Generally, specific regions are subdivided into sites, normally administered and excavated by different groups. Each site is further subdivided into partitions, sub-partitions, and loci, the latter being the nucleus of the excavation. Materials or artifacts found in different loci are organized in containers for further reference and analysis. The locus is the elementary volume unit used for establishing archaeological relationships. Archaeological relationships between loci are from both the vertical and horizontal points of view. The first is given by reference to loci above and below a given locus, the second by coexisting loci (loci located at the same level). The archaeological relationship is related to the temporal succession of various events of construction, deposition, and destruction. Temporal sequencing of archaeological items involves linking items to form a stratigraphic diagram of the kind developed in the 1970s by Edward Harris (http://www.harrismatrix.com/) and now used by many archaeologists. A "Harris Matrix" is a compact diagram representing the essential stratigraphic relationships among all the items; it shows the chronological relationship between excavated layers and contexts. In general, if two layers are in contact with each other and one lies over the other, then the upper layer is chronologically later. This is the basis on which the structural history of a site is founded. The construction of this diagram and its subsequent use in the interpretation of structural phases is central to both the understanding of the site during excavation and to post-excavation analysis [22]. Spatial and stratigraphic relationships among archaeological items can be regarded as extrinsic attributes (inter-item relationships) [102]; intrinsic attributes are those describing the items themselves. Finally, since archaeological information is highly variable, items observed in a typical excavation may fall into a wide variety of different classification systems, and may exhibit many idiosyncrasies.

5. Streams

In an archaeological setting, streams represent the enormous amount of dynamic multimedia information generated in the processes of planning, excavating, analyzing, and publishing. Examples include photos and drawings of excavation sites, loci, or unearthed artifacts; audio and video recordings of excavation activities; textual reports; and 3D models used to reconstruct and visualize archaeological ruins.

With key requirements for ArchDLs summarized above and in "Requirements Gathering and Modeling of Domain-Specific Digital Libraries with the 5S Framework: An Archaelogical Case Study with ETANA" [104], we can proceed to constructively define a minimal ArchDL metamodel. A domain-specific metamodel is a generic model which captures aspects specific to the domain at hand. We build upon the definition of a minimal DL and extend it with concepts specific to the archaeology domain. Following our minimalist approach, we only define essential concepts without which we think a DL cannot be considered an ArchDL as described in Appendix C of Book 1 of this series (see also [104]).

In this section we use the 5SGraph tool [124, 125] to specify two of the archaeological information systems of ETANA projects (http://www.etana.org/).

Fig. 2.5 illustrates the use of 5SGraph to specify the Nimrin archaeological site, focusing on Structure, drawing upon a metamodel for archaeology that we have built for ETANA-DL [87, 88, 89]. Nimrin has three metadata catalogs, and each has its corresponding metadata format as described in its local schema. The scenario model for the Halif site only consists of a database searching service as shown in Fig. 2.6, while ETANA-DL has eight main services (see Fig. 2.7). In Section 2.3.2, we present how to integrate various structure models into the one for the union DL using a visual mapping tool.

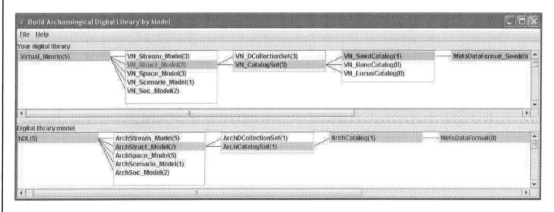

Figure 2.5: Structure model for Nimrin [103, 104, 106].

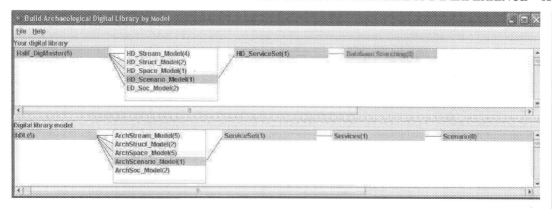

Figure 2.6: Scenario model for Halif [103, 104, 106].

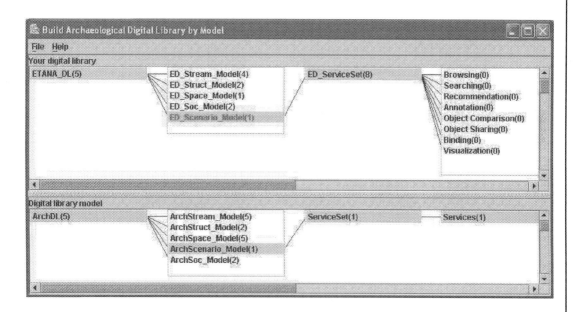

Figure 2.7: Scenario model for ETANA-DL [103, 104, 106].

2.3.2   VISUAL MAPPING TOOL: SCHEMAMAPPER

Semantic interoperability is of primary importance in DL integration. The intermediary-based approach and the mapping-based approach are interrelated as shown in Fig. 2.2. The mapping-based approach attempts to construct mappings between semantically related information sources. It is usually accomplished by constructing a global schema and by establishing mappings between that global schema and each local schema. In this section, we present an incremental approach through intermediary- and mapping-based techniques and a visual mapping tool, SchemaMapper.

Features of SchemaMapper

Schema mapping is an interesting problem that usually has been addressed from either an algorithmic point of view or from a visualization point of view. SchemaMapper combines these two perspectives as follows.

1. Algorithmic perspective

Mapping recommendations by SchemaMapper consist of name-based (e.g., using edit distance), rule-based, and mapping history-based strategies.

2. Visualization perspective

SchemaMapper presents local and global schemas using hyperbolic trees [83, 84]. This allows more nodes to be displayed than with linear representation techniques, and avoids the problem of scrolling. Though full node names cannot be displayed (to conserve space), these are available as tool-tip information on individual nodes. Different colors are assigned to differentiate between root level, leaf, non-leaf, recommended, and mapped nodes (with a color legend present on the lower right of Fig. 2.8). A table that contains a list of all the mappings in the current session is shown at the bottom left of the screen in Fig. 2.8. Users may or may not choose to accept recommendations.

SchemaMapper allows global schema editing: deleting nodes, renaming nodes, and adding a local schema sub-tree to the global schema. This has special value for many DLs, e.g., ArchDLs, where it is impossible to predict the final global schema because of its evolutionary nature. SchemaMapper may be superior in this respect to commercial mapping tools like MapForce (http://www.altova.com/mapforce.html) which lack schema editing capabilities. As a global schema evolves, in order to preserve consistency in the naming of semantically similar nodes, SchemaMapper recommends appropriate name changes to global schema nodes, based on the history stored in a mapping database.

Once the local schema has been mapped to the global schema, an XSLT [14] style sheet containing the mapping is produced by SchemaMapper. This style sheet is essentially the wrapper containing the mappings. When applied to a collection of XML files conforming to the local schema, the style sheet transforms those files to ones conforming to the global schema. The transformed files can be harvested into a union DL. SchemaMapper also saves any changes made to the global schema, and updates the mapping database.

Archaeological DL Application

During the past several decades, archaeology as a discipline and practice has increasingly embraced digital technologies and electronic resources. Vast quantities of heterogeneous data are generated, stored, and processed by customized monolithic information systems. Migration or export of ar-

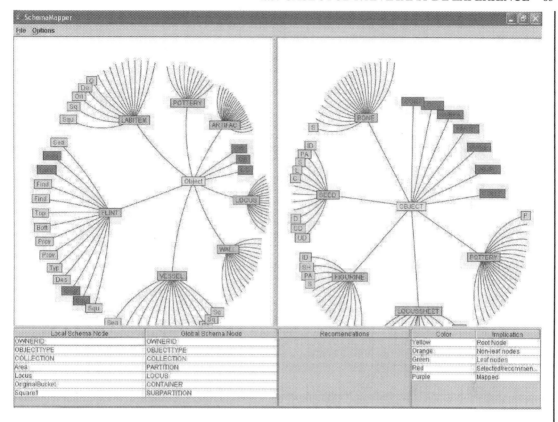

Figure 2.8: Initial set of mappings for flint tool based on rules and name-based matching [83, 103, 104, 106].

chaeological data from one system to another is a monumental task that is aggravated by peculiar data formats and database schemas. Furthermore, archaeological data classification depends on a number of vaguely defined qualitative characteristics, which are open to personal interpretation. Different branches of archaeology have special methods of classification; progress in digs and new types of excavated finds makes it impossible to foresee an ultimate global schema for the description of all excavation data [22]. Accordingly, an "incremental" approach is desired for global schema enrichment.

In this section, we explain how all these DL integration requirements can be satisfied, through semi-automatic wrapper generation based on SchemaMapper that continuously improves the global schema. Through the integration of artifact data from the Megiddo excavation site into ETANA-DL, we demonstrate that SchemaMapper allows semi-automatic mapping and incremental global schema enrichment, and supports union catalog generation for a union DL.

Megiddo is widely regarded as the most important archaeological site in Israel from Biblical times, and as one of the most significant sites for the study of the ancient Near East. The excavation data collection we received from Megiddo is stored in more than ten database tables containing over 30,000 records with seven different types, namely wall, locus, pottery bucket, flint tool, vessel, lab item, and miscellaneous artifact. The Megiddo schema is described in a structure sub-model within the 5S framework. Structures represent the way archaeological information is organized along several dimensions; it is spatially organized, temporally sequenced, and highly variable. The Megiddo site organization is shown in Fig. 2.9.

Megiddo overview

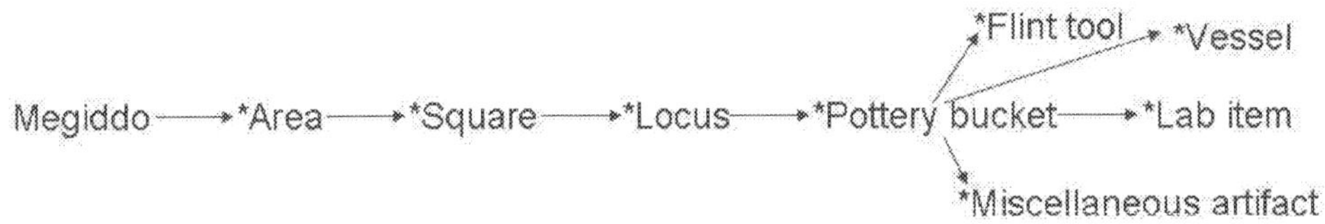

Figure 2.9: Megiddo site organization [83, 103, 104, 106].

Scenario for mapping Megiddo schema into ETANA-DL global schema

As described earlier, the Megiddo collection consists of seven different types of artifacts. For integrating it into ETANA-DL, we produce one mapping style sheet per artifact. In the following scenarios, we first consider the mapping of "flint tool," and then use the knowledge of this mapping to help map "vessel."

The left-hand side of Fig. 2.8 shows the Megiddo local schema, while the right-hand side shows the ETANA-DL global schema. The ETANA-DL global schema contains the BONE, SEED, FIGURINE, LOCUSSHEET, and POTTERY artifacts already included, apart from the top-level leaf nodes (OWNERID, OBJECTTYPE, COLLECTION, PARTITION, SUBPARTITION, LOCUS, and CONTAINER) that would be presented in all artifacts.

Based on rules and name based matching strategies, SchemaMapper recommends mappings: OWNERID → OWNERID, OBJECTTYPE → OBJECTTYPE, COLLECTION → COLLECTION, Area → PARTITION, Square1 → SUBPARTITION, Locus → LOCUS, and OriginalBucket → CONTAINER. (OWNERID, OBJECTTYPE, and COLLECTION are top-level leaf-nodes whereas Area, Square1, Locus, and OriginalBucket are all elements of the schema of the flint tool collection.)

The above mapping format has the local schema node on the left-hand side and the recommended global schema node on the right-hand side. We map the nodes according to the recommendations, indicated by coloring these nodes purple (see Fig. 2.8).

As the remaining nodes in the local schema do not have corresponding global schema nodes, we add the flint tool sub-tree as a child of the OBJECT node in the global schema. This ensures that local schema elements and properties are preserved during the mapping transformation. SchemaMapper determines that some of the nodes (Area, Locus, OriginalBucket, and Square1) are already mapped, deletes these nodes from the global schema sub-tree, and automatically maps the rest with the corresponding elements in the local sub-tree (see Fig. 2.10). The user may decide to rename some nodes in the global schema from within this sub-tree to avoid any local connections with the name. Assume the user renames global schema node "Description" to "DESCRIPTION." With this the mapping process is complete (see Fig. 2.10). Once the user decides to confirm the mappings, a style sheet is generated, the mappings are stored in the database, and the ETANA-DL global schema is updated with the flint tool schema.

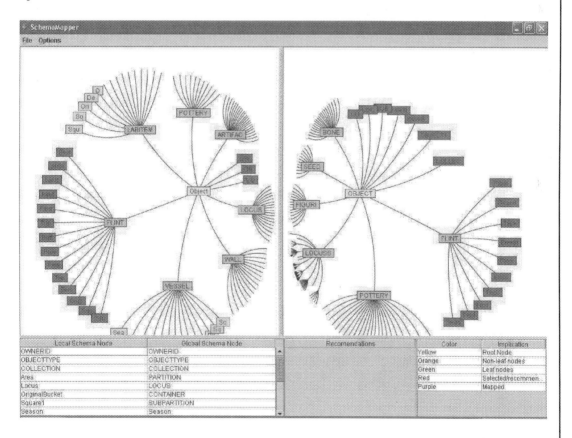

Figure 2.10: Adding FLINT sub-tree as a child of OBJECT in the global schema [83, 103, 104, 106].

We next integrate the schema of VESSEL artifacts of Megiddo into the ETANA-DL global schema. When we open the global schema for mapping, along with the other artifacts, the flint tool, which was integrated in the previous step, also is present (see Fig. 2.10). From the mapping of the flint tool we realize that mapping of a completely new artifact requires only the top-level leaf nodes to be displayed in the global schema. For integration of a completely new artifact, the user may choose to view only the top-level leaf nodes in order to avoid erroneous cross mappings from schema nodes of one of the artifacts to similar schema nodes present in other artifacts (see Figs. 2.11 and 2.12). This prevents the user from accidentally modifying a node, from say the flint tool sub-tree in the global schema, and rendering the previously generated XML files inconsistent. Also, this avoids confusing the user, by presenting him with only the information he needs to see for mapping. Once again recommendations are made to enable the initial set of seven mappings; after this, the user adds the VESSEL sub-tree to the global schema.

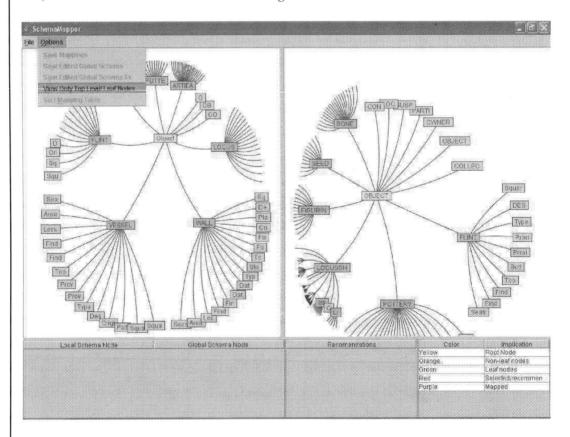

Figure 2.11: Using the View Only Top Leaf Nodes option mapping Vessel Collection [83, 103, 104, 106].

As before, SchemaMapper finds that the Area, Locus, Square1, and Original-Bucket nodes are already mapped—and deletes them in the global sub-tree, and then maps the remaining nodes to corresponding local schema nodes automatically. SchemaMapper also goes through the mappings history and finds that the Description node in the flint tool sub-tree was mapped to the DESCRIP-TION node in the global schema. In order to keep naming consistent, Schema Mapper recommends the user to change the name of the Description node in the VESSEL sub-tree to DESCRIPTION (see Fig. 2.12). This is due to the fact that both the DESCRIPTION node in the flint tool sub-

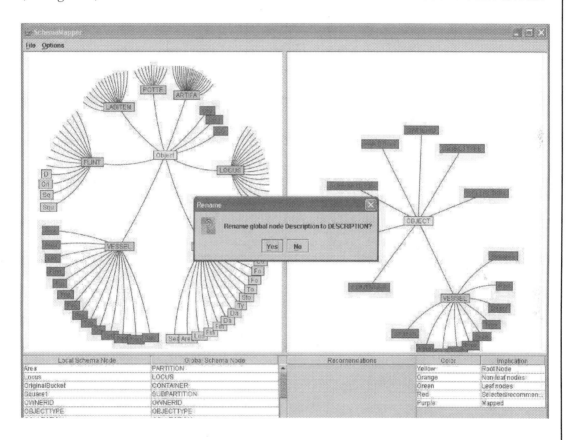

Figure 2.12: Name change recommendation based on mapping history [83, 103, 104, 106].

branch of the global schema and the Description node in the VESSEL sub-branch of the global schema describe the same artifact type, but as DESCRIPTION has been selected as the global name, all Description elements in the global sub-tree should be renamed as DESCRIPTION. The recommendation, as always, is not mandatory, but if followed will help keep names consistent. When the user confirms the mappings, the database is updated, the style sheet generated, and the global schema updated with the VESSEL schema. It is important to note that the integration of vessel artifacts into the global schema in no way changed the existing flint global entry. This leads us to the observation that, for Megiddo, modification of the global schema is simply appending a new local artifact into the global schema without changing the existing artifacts in the global schema.

The style sheets generated are applied on each sub-collection of Megiddo (like vessel or flint tool collection) to convert each local collection to one conforming to the global schema. Transformed collections are ready for harvest into the union catalog in ETANA-DL, and are available for access by services like Searching and Browsing.

2.4   SUMMARY

In this chapter, we apply the 5S framework to integrate domain-specific (archaeological) DLs, illustrating our solutions for key problems in DL integration. An integrated Archaeological DL, ETANA-DL, is used as a case study to demonstrate and allow evaluation of our DL integration approach.

2.5   EXERCISES AND PROJECTS

1. Which of the integration problems described in this chapter are exclusive to digital libraries, and not commonly found when integrating databases?

2. What kind of intermediary-based approach is used by commercial search engines to deal with information integration?

3. What are some good examples of integrated services in a DL? How is each one of those services changed to make it integrated?

4. How would the approach to requirements identification that was described for archaeology be applied in another domain of particular interest to you? What are the results of that process for each of the 5Ss?

5. In some circumstances, the federation approach continues to be used rather than a harvesting-based approach. Pick one of those, and describe the key reasons that motivate use of federation. Explain the resulting benefits as well as any remaining challenges or difficulties that come from choosing federation.

6. Sometimes situations in which harvesting is chosen rather than federation lead to a "dumbing down" in the case of one or more services. Give an example of such a situation. Explain in what regard there has been some "dumbing down." What is the reason that this type of solution was adopted instead of a solution that achieves a more appropriate integration with fewer losses?

7. Sometimes situations in which federation is chosen rather than harvesting lead to a "dumbing down" in the case of one or more services. Give an example of such a situation. Explain in what regard there has been some "dumbing down." What is the reason that this type of solution was adopted instead of a solution that achieves a more appropriate integration with fewer losses?

8. In recent years there has been an increased use of digital libraries in mobile environments. Pick one such new DL application in which the approach to integration is much effected because of the mobile solution. Describe what is different in a mobile setting from what is deployed for users who work on a desktop in an office.

9. In the business world, mergers and acquisitions have led to changes in information systems so there is integration of the information system of both the company that has been acquired, and of the new larger company. Pick one such corporate situation and describe the key changes that have been made to achieve integration. Referring to Fig. 2.1, explain at a high level the approach adopted. Give additional explantion, referring to Fig. 2.2.

10. The Open Archives Initiative Protocol for Metadata Harvesting has been employed in a number of DLs to aid in integration. Pick one such DL integration effort not explicitly discussed in this chapter, with which you have familiarity, or that you can find in the published literature. Describe how OAI-PMH has helped with the integration, explaining the benefits. Also, discuss the key limitations of this approach, and any problems resulting from the approach chosen.

11. Many challenges to integration result from the use of a crosswalk that is particularly complicated. Pick one example of integration involving such a crosswalk. Explain the main advantages and main disadvantages.

12. Consider the mapping approach discussed in this chapter. How might this approach be adapted in a setting where a local schema must be adapted to fit with the global schema, where the local schema is described using a different natural language?

13. Often, when a wrapper-based approach is chosen for integration, information is represented in both an original form and in the transformed representation. Give an example of where this is particularly problematic. Explain the main problems that remain and are hard to solve.

14. When a large and complex ontology is used in an integrated DL, and when digital objects have not been related to that ontology, but have been related to a much simpler taxonomy, there may be a number of challenges that must be addressed. Describe one such situation. Explain the key problems faced, and the solution adopted. What are the advantages and disadvantages of this approach?

15. Give another example of an approach to vertical search similar to the Yahoo! SERP example given. Explain how it is similar to what is discussed in this chapter. Explain how it is different. Explain the pros and cons relative to what is considered in the chapter.

16. Some integrated services have been discussed in this chapter. What other DL service can be seen in an integrated DL, that is not discussed, but yet is changed in some significant way because of integration? What are the pros and cons of the solution adopted to integrate that service?

17. Pick some aspect of DL integration that has not been formally described in this chapter. Building upon the discussion in this chapter and in the prior book in the series, add to the formalisms given, to characterize the aspect of concern. Explain how the 5S framework has helped, or made more difficult, this formal approach.

Bibliography

[1] N. Adam, V. Atluri, and I. Adiwijaya. Systems integration in digital libraries. *Commun. ACM*, 43(6):64–72, 2000. DOI: 10.1145/336460.336476 49

[2] B. Alexe, L. Chiticariu, R. J. Miller, and W. C. Tan. Mapping understanding and design by example. In *ICDE 2008*, pages 10–19, 2008. DOI: 10.1109/ICDE.2008.4497409 57

[3] B. Alexe, B. ten Cate, P. G. Kolaitis, and W.-C. Tan. Designing and refining schema mappings via data examples. In *SIGMOD 2011*, pages 133–144, 2011. DOI: 10.1145/1989323.1989338 57, 58

[4] R. Amsler. Application of citation-based automatic classification. Technical report, The University of Texas at Austin, Linguistics Research Center, December 1972. 15

[5] W. Arms, D. Hillmann, C. Lagoze, D. Krafft, R. Marisa, J. Saylor, and C. Terrizzi. A spectrum of interoperability: The site for science prototype for the NSDL. *D-Lib Magazine*, 8(1), 2002. DOI: 10.1045/january2002-arms 50

[6] E. Babbie. *The Practice of Social Research*. Wadsworth Publishing Company, Belmont, California, 6th edition, 1990. 4

[7] R. Baeza-Yates and B. Ribeiro-Neto. *Modern Information Retrieval*. Addison-Wesley, Harlow, England, 1999. 14, 23

[8] A. Balog. Testing a multidimensional and hierarchical quality assessment model for digital libraries. *Studies in Informatics and Control*, 20(3):233–246, 2011. 3

[9] N. Belkin. Anomalous states of knowledge as the basis for information retrieval. *Canadian Journal of Inf. Sci.*, 5:133–143, 1980. 58

[10] N. Belkin, P. Marchetti, and C. Cool. BRAQUE: Design of an interface to support user interaction in information retrieval. *Information Processing and Management*, 29(3):325–344, 1993. DOI: 10.1016/0306-4573(93)90059-M 58

[11] C. M. Bowman, P. B. Danzig, D. R. Hardy, U. Manber, and M. F. Schwartz. The Harvest information discovery and access system. *Computer Networks and ISDN Systems*, 28(1):119–126, 1995. DOI: 10.1016/0169-7552(95)00098-5 57

[12] L. Candela, D. Castelli, N. Ferro, Y. Ioannidis, G. Koutrika, C. Meghini, P. Pagano, S. Ross, D. Soergel, M. Agosti, M. Dobreva, V. Katifori, and H. Schuldt. The DELOS Digital Library Reference Model - Foundations for Digital Libraries. Version 0.98, 2008. `http://www.delos.info/files/pdf/ReferenceModel/DELOS%5FDLReferenceModel%5F0.98.pdf` [last visited July 4, 2012]. 2, 3

[13] CITIDEL. Computing and Information Technology Interactive Digital Educational Library, www.citidel.org, 2004. 33

[14] J. Clark. XSL transformations (XSLT), Version 1.0, W3C Recommendation 16 November, 1999. 64

[15] E. Cosijn and P. Ingwersen. Dimensions of relevance. *Inf. Process. Manage.*, 36(4):533–550, 2000. DOI: 10.1016/S0306-4573(99)00072-2 13

[16] T. Couto, M. Cristo, M. A. Gonçalves, P. Calado, N. Ziviani, E. Moura, and B. Ribeiro-Neto. A comparative study of citations and links in document classification. In *Proceedings of the 6th ACM/IEEE-CS joint conference on digital libraries*, pages 75–84, New York, NY, USA, 2006. ACM Press. DOI: 10.1145/1141753.1141766 43

[17] A. Crespo and H. Garcia-Molina. Archival storage for digital libraries. In *DL'98: Proceedings of the 3rd ACM International Conference on Digital Libraries*, pages 69–78, 1998. DOI: 10.1145/276675.276683 10

[18] F. A. Das Neves. *Stepping Stones and Pathways:Improving Retrieval by Chains of Relationships between Documents*. Doctoral dissertation, Virginia Tech, 2004. 58

[19] M. Dean, D. Connolly, F. Van-Harmelen, J. Hendler, I. Horrocks, D. McGuinness, P. Patel-Schneider, and L. Stein. OWL Web Ontology Language 1.0 Reference. Internet `http://www.w3.org/TR/owl-ref/`, 2002. 55

[20] F. Diaz. Integration of news content into web results. In *WSDM'09*, pages 182–191, 2009. DOI: 10.1145/1498759.1498825 55

[21] A. Doan, J. Madhavan, R. Dhamankar, et al. Learning to match ontologies on the Semantic Web. *VLDB Journal: Very Large Data Bases*, 12(4):303–319, Nov. 2003. DOI: 10.1007/s00778-003-0104-2 57

[22] I. Finkelstein, D. Ussishkin, and B. Halpern. *Megiddo III: The 1992-1996 Seasons*. Monograph Series of the Institute of Archaeology. Tel Aviv University No. 18, 2000. 61, 65

[23] D. J. Foskett. A note on the concept of relevance. *Information Storage and Retrieval*, 8(2):77–78, 1972. DOI: 10.1016/0020-0271(72)90009-5 13

[24] E. Fox and R. France. Architecture of an expert system for composite document analysis, representation and retrieval. *International Journal of Approximate Reasoning*, 1(2):151–175, 1987. DOI: 10.1016/0888-613X(87)90012-0 58

[25] E. Fox, R. France, E. Sahle, A. Daoud, and B. Cline. Development of a Modern OPAC: From REVTOLC to MARIAN. In *Proc. 16th Annual Intern'l ACM SIGIR Conf. on R & D in Information Retrieval, SIGIR '93, Pittsburgh, PA, June 27 - July 1*, pages 248–259, 1993. DOI: 10.1145/160688.160730 58

[26] E. Fox, G. McMillan, H. Suleman, M. Gonçalves, and M. Luo. Networked Digital Library of Theses and Dissertations (NDLTD). In J. Andrews and D. Law, editors, *Digital Libraries: Policy, Planning and Practice*, chapter 11, pages 167–187. Ashgate Publishing, Hants, England, 2004. 5

[27] E. A. Fox, Y. Chen, M. Akbar, C. A. Shaffer, S. H. Edwards, P. Brusilovsky, D. D. Garcia, L. M. Delcambre, F. Decker, D. W. Archer, R. Furuta, F. Shipman, S. Carpenter, and L. Cassel. Ensemble PDP-8: Eight Principles for Distributed Portals. In *Proc. JCDL/ICADL 2010, June 21-25, Gold Coast, Australia*, pages 341–344. ACM, 2010. DOI: 10.1145/1816123.1816174 54

[28] E. A. Fox, D. Knox, L. Cassel, J. A. N. Lee, M. Pérez-Quiñones, J. Impagliazzo, and C. L. Giles. CITIDEL: Computing and Information Technology Interactive Digital Educational Library, 2002. http://www.citidel.org [last visited July 4, 2012]. 5

[29] E. A. Fox and G. Marchionini. Toward a worldwide digital library. *Communications of the ACM*, 41(4):22–28, 1998. DOI: 10.1145/273035.273043 48

[30] E. A. Fox, F. Neves, X. Yu, R. Shen, S. Kim, and W. Fan. Exploring the computing literature with visualization and stepping stones and pathways. *Commun. ACM*, 49(4):52–58, 2006. DOI: 10.1145/1121949.1121982 58

[31] N. Fuhr, P. Hansen, M. Mabe, A. Micsik, and I. Solvberg. Digital libraries: A generic classification and evaluation scheme. *Lecture Notes in Computer Science*, 2163:187, 2001. DOI: 10.1007/3-540-44796-2_17 1, 2

[32] N. Fuhr, G. Tsakonas, T. Aalberg, M. Agosti, P. Hansen, S. Kapidakis, C.-P. Klas, L. Kovas, M. Landoni, A. Micsik, C. Papatheodorou, C. Peters, and I. Solvberg. Evaluation of digital libraries. *International Journal of Digital Libraries*, 8(1):21–38, 2007. DOI: 10.1007/s00799-007-0011-z 2

[33] G. Furnas and S. Rauch. Considerations for Information Environments and the NaviQue Workspace. In *Proceedings of ACM Digital Libraries 1998*, pages 79–88, 1998. http://sr-hercules01.iat.sfu.ca/CzSawVA/images/2/28/Furnas%5Fnavique.pdf [last visited July 4, 2012]. DOI: 10.1145/276675.276684 58

76 BIBLIOGRAPHY

[34] G. Golovchinsky. Queries? links? is there a difference? In *Proc. CHI'97*, pages 407–417, 1997. DOI: 10.1145/258549.258820 58

[35] M. A. Gonçalves. *Streams, Structures, Spaces, Scenarios, and Societies (5S): A Formal Digital Library Framework and Its Applications*. Ph.D. thesis, Virginia Tech, Blacksburg, VA, 2004. `http://scholar.lib.vt.edu/theses/available/etd-12052004-135923/` [last visited July 4, 2012]. xxi, 48

[36] M. A. Gonçalves, E. A. Fox, L. T. Watson, and N. A. Kipp. Streams, structures, spaces, scenarios, societies (5S): A formal model for digital libraries. *ACM Transactions on Information Systems*, 22(2):270–312, 2004. DOI: 10.1145/984321.984325 18, 48, 60

[37] M. A. Gonçalves, R. K. France, and E. A. Fox. MARIAN: Flexible Interoperability for Federated Digital Libraries. *Springer Lecture Notes in Computer Science*, 2163:173–186, 2001. `http://link.springer-ny.com/link/service/series/0558/bibs/2163/21630173.htm` [last visited July 4, 2012]. DOI: 10.1007/3-540-44796-2_16 55

[38] M. A. Gonçalves, M. Luo, R. Shen, M. F. Ali, and E. A. Fox. An XML log standard and tool for digital library logging analysis. In *Research and Advanced Technology for Digital Libraries, 6th European Conference, ECDL 2002, Rome, Italy, September 16-18, 2002, Proceedings, eds. Maristella Agosti and Constantino Thanos, LNCS 2458, Springer*, pages 129–143, 2002. DOI: 10.1007/3-540-45747-X_10 27

[39] M. A. Gonçalves, B. L. Moreira, E. A. Fox, and L. T. Watson. What is a good digital library? - defining a quality model for digital libraries. *Information Processing & Management*, 43(5):1416–1437, 2007. DOI: 10.1016/j.ipm.2006.11.010 26

[40] M. A. Gonçalves, G. Panchanathan, U. Ravindranathan, A. Krowne, E. A. Fox, F. Jagodzinski, and L. Cassel. The XML log standard for digital libraries: Analysis, evolution, and deployment. In *Proc. JCDL'2003, Third ACM / IEEE-CS Joint Conference on Digital Libraries, May 27-31, Houston, TX*, pages 312–314. ACM, 2003. DOI: 10.1109/JCDL.2003.1204933 2, 27

[41] G. Gottlob and P. Senellart. Schema mapping discovery from data instances. *J. ACM*, 57(2):334–350, 2010. DOI: 10.1145/1667053.1667055 57

[42] H. Greisdorf. Relevance thresholds: a multi-stage predictive model of how users evaluate information. *Information Processing and Management*, 39(3):403–423, 2003. DOI: 10.1016/S0306-4573(02)00032-8 9

[43] N. Guarino, D. Oberle, and S. Staab. What is an ontology? In S. Staab and R. Studer, editors, *Handbook on Ontologies*, International Handbooks on Information Systems, pages 1–17. Springer Berlin Heidelberg, 2009. DOI: 10.1007/978-3-540-92673-3 54

[44] J. V. Hansen. Audit considerations in distributed processing systems. *Communications of the ACM*, 26(8):562–569, 1983. DOI: 10.1145/358161.358166 25

[45] D. Harman. *Information Retrieval Evaluation*. Morgan and Claypool Publishers, series ed. Gary Marchionini, 2011. DOI: 10.2200/S00368ED1V01Y201105ICR019 1

[46] W. Hasselbring. Information System Integration: Introduction. *Commun. ACM*, 43(6):32–38, 2000. DOI: 10.1145/336460.336472 47

[47] J. Hunter and S. Choudhury. A semi-automated digital preservation system based on semantic web services. In *Proceedings of the Fourth ACM/IEEE-CS Joint Conference on Digital Libraries*, pages 269–278, Tucson, Arizona, 2004. DOI: 10.1109/JCDL.2004.1336136 10, 12

[48] J. Impagliazzo. Using CITIDEL as a Portal for CS Education. In *CCSCNE Conference*, 2002. Panel Presentation and Chair (with L. Cassel and D. Knox). 33

[49] P. Ingwersen, K. van Rijsbergen, and N. Belkin. Context in Information Retrieval. `http:// ir.dcs.gla.ac.uk/context/IRinContext_WorkshopNotes_SIGIR2004.pdf`, 2004. 9

[50] P. Innocenti, G. Vullo, and S. Ross. Towards a digital library policy and quality interoperability framework: the DL.org project. *New Review of Information Networking*, 15(1):29–53, 2010. DOI: 10.1080/13614571003751071 3

[51] P. G. Ipeirotis and L. Gravano. Distributed search over the hidden Web: hierarchical database sampling and selection. In *Proceedings of the 28th Int. Conference on Very Large Data Bases, Hong Kong SAR, China, 20–23 August 2002*, pages 394–405, 2002. 20

[52] K. Järvelin and J. Kekäläinen. Cumulated gain-based evaluation of IR techniques. *ACM Transactions on Information Systems*, 20(20):422–446, 2002. DOI: 10.1145/582415.582418 1

[53] N. Kampanya, R. Shen, S. Kim, C. North, and E. A. Fox. CitiViz: A visual user interface to the CITIDEL system. In *Proc. European Conference on Digital Libraries (ECDL) 2004, September 12-17, University of Bath, UK*. Springer, 2004. DOI: 10.1007/978-3-540-30230-8_12 58

[54] D. A. Kemp. Relevance, pertinence, and information system development. *Information Storage and Retrieval*, 10(2):37–47, 1974. DOI: 10.1016/0020-0271(74)90002-3 13

[55] M. M. Kessler. Bibliographic coupling between scientific papers. *American Documentation*, 14(1):10–25, 1963. DOI: 10.1002/asi.5090140103 15, 42

[56] M. Khoo and C. MacDonald. An organizational model for digital library evaluation. In *TPDL'11 Proceedings of the 15th international conference on Theory and practice of digital libraries: research and advanced technology for digital libraries*, pages 329–340, 2011. DOI: 10.1007/978-3-642-24469-8_34 4

[57] C.-P. Klas, N. Fuhr, S. Kriewel, H. Albrechtsen, G. Tsakonas, S. Kapidakis, C. Papatheodorou, P. Hansen, L. Kovacs, A. Micsik, and E. Jacob. An experimental framework for comparative digital library evaluation: the logging scheme. In *Proceedings of the 6th ACM/IEEE-CS joint conference on digital libraries*, pages 308–309, New York, NY, USA, 2006. ACM Press. DOI: 10.1145/1141753.1141822 2

[58] S. R. Kruk and B. McDaniel. *Semantic Digital Libraries.* Springer, 2009. DOI: 10.1007/978-3-540-85434-0 51

[59] M. Kyrillidou and S. Giersch. Developing the DigiQUAL protocol for digital library evaluation. In *JCDL '05: Proceedings of the 5th ACM/IEEE-CS joint conference on digital libraries*, pages 172–173, New York, NY, USA, 2005. ACM Press. DOI: 10.1145/1065385.1065426 2

[60] A. H. F. Laender, M. A. Gonçalves, and P. A. Roberto. BDBComp: building a digital library for the Brazilian computer science community. In *Proceedings of the 4th ACM/IEEE-CS joint conference on digital libraries*, pages 23–24, New York, NY, USA, 2004. ACM Press. DOI: 10.1145/996350.996357 33, 38

[61] B. Lagoeiro, M. A. Gonçalves, and E. A. Fox. 5SQual: A quality tool for digital libraries. In *Proceedings of the 7th ACM/IEEE Joint Conference on Digital Libraries*, page (demonstration accepted), New York, NY, USA, 2007. ACM Press. DOI: 10.1145/1255175.1255313 3, 4

[62] C. Lagoze, W. Arms, S. Gan, D. Hillmann, C. Ingram, D. Krafft, R. Marisa, J. Phipps, J. Saylor, C. Terrizzi, W. Hoehn, D. Millman, J. Allan, S. Guzman-Lara, and Kalt. Core services in the architecture of the National Science Digital Library (NSDL). In *JCDL'02: Proceedings of the 2nd ACM/IEEE-CS Joint Conference on Digital Libraries, Houston, TX*, pages 201–209, 2002. DOI: 10.1145/544220.544264 48

[63] R. L. Larsen and H. D. Wactlar. *Knowledge Lost in Information: Report of the NSF Workshop on Research Directions for Digital Libraries, June 15-17, 2003, Chatham, MA.* University of Pittsburgh, Pittsburgh, 2004. 51

[64] D. M. Levy. Heroic measures: reflections on the possibility and purpose of digital preservation. In *DL'98: Proceedings of the 3rd ACM International Conference on Digital Libraries*, pages 152–161, Pittsburgh, PA, 1998. DOI: 10.1145/276675.276692 10

[65] X. Liu, K. Maly, M. Zubair, and M. L. Nelson. Arc - an OAI service provider for digital library federation. *D-Lib Magazine*, 7(4), 2001. April. DOI: 10.1045/april2001-liu 55

[66] R. A. Lorie. A methodology and system for preserving digital data. In *JCDL 2002*, pages 312–319, Portland, Oregon, 2002. ACM. DOI: 10.1145/544220.544296 10

[67] G. Marchionini. *Information Seeking in Electronic Environments.* Cambridge University Press, Cambridge, 1995. DOI: 10.1017/CBO9780511626388 58

[68] G. Marchionini. Evaluating digital libraries: a longitudinal and multifaceted view. *Library Trends*, 49(2):304–333, 2000. 2

[69] G. Marchionini, C. Plaisant, and A. Komlodi. The people in digital libraries: multifaceted approaches to assessing needs and impact. In A. P. Biship, editor, *Digital Library Use: Social Practice in Design and Evaluation*, pages 119–160. The MIT Press, 2003. 2, 3

[70] S. Mizzaro. A cognitive analysis of information retrieval. In *Information Science: Integration in Perspective – Proceedings of CoLIS2*, pages 233–250, Copenhagen, Denmark, 1996. 9

[71] S. Mizzaro. How many relevances in information retrieval? *Interacting With Computers*, 10(3):305–322, 1998. DOI: 10.1016/S0953-5438(98)00012-5 9

[72] NDLTD. Networked Digital Library of Theses and Dissertations. http://www.ndltd. org, 2004. 5

[73] OAI. OAI-PMH - open archives initiative protocol for metadata harvesting - v.2.0. http:// www.openarchives.org/OAI/openarchivesprotocol.html, 2001. 27, 50, 57

[74] A. Paepcke, R. Brandriff, G. Janee, R. Larson, B. Ludaescher, S. Melnik, and S. Raghavan. Search middleware and the simple digital library interoperability protocol. *D-Lib Magazine*, 6(3), 2000. March. DOI: 10.1045/march2000-paepcke 49

[75] A. Paepcke, C.-C. K. Chang, T. Winograd, and H. Garcia-Molina. Interoperability for Digital Libraries Worldwide. *Communications of the ACM*, 41(4):33–42, 1998. DOI: 10.1145/273035.273044 49

[76] J. Park and S. Ram. Information systems interoperability: What lies beneath? *ACM Transactions on Information Systems (TOIS)*, 22(4):595–632, 2004. DOI: 10.1145/1028099.1028103 50, 51

[77] M. Patel, T. Koch, M. Doerr, and C. Tsinaraki. *Semantic Interoperability in Digital Library Systems: Report of DELOS2 Network of Excellence in Digital Libraries.* DELOS, 2005. 51

[78] S. Payette, C. Blanchi, C. Lagoze, and E. A. Overly. Interoperability for digital objects and repositories: The Cornell/CNRI experiments. *D-Lib Magazine*, 5(5), 1999. May. DOI: 10.1045/may99-payette 49

[79] S. F. Pileggi and C. Fernandez-Llatas. *Semantic Interoperability: Issues, Solutions, Challenges.* River Publishers, 2012. 51

[80] L. L. Pipino, Y. W. Lee, and R. Y. Wang. Data quality assessment. *Communications of the ACM*, 45(4):211–218, 2002. DOI: 10.1145/505248.506010 15

[81] A. K. Ponnuswami, K. Pattabiraman, D. Brand, and T. Kanungo. Model characterization curves for federated search using click-logs: Predicting user engagement metrics for the span of feasible operating points. In *WWW'11*, pages 67–76, 2011. DOI: 10.1145/1963405.1963419 55

[82] J. Powell and E. A. Fox. Multilingual federated searching across heterogeneous collections. *D-Lib Magazine*, 5(8), 1998. DOI: 10.1045/september98-powell 55

[83] A. Raghavan, D. Rangarajan, R. Shen, M. Goncalves, N. Vemuri, W. Fan, and E. A. Fox. Schema Mapper: A visualization tool for DL integration. In *JCDL'05: Proceedings of the 5th ACM/IEEE-CS Joint Conference on Digital Libraries*, pages 414–414, 2005. DOI: 10.1145/1065385.1065518 xvi, 64, 65, 66, 67, 68, 69

[84] A. Raghavan, N. S. Vemuri, R. Shen, M. A. Gonçalves, W. Fan, and E. A. Fox. Incremental, semi-automatic, mapping-based integration of heterogeneous collections into archaeological digital libraries: Megiddo case study. In *ECDL'05: Proceedings of the 5th European Conference on Digital Libraries*, pages 139–150, 2005. DOI: 10.1007/11551362_13 64

[85] E. Rahm and P. Bernstein. A Survey of Approaches to Automatic Schema Matching. *VLDB Journal*, 10(4):334–350, 2001. DOI: 10.1007/s007780100057 58

[86] S. Ram, J. Park, and D. Lee. Digital libraries for the next millennium: Challenges and research directions. *Information Systems Frontiers*, 1(1):75–94, 1999. DOI: 10.1023/A:1010021029890 49

[87] U. Ravindranathan. Prototyping Digital Libraries Handling Heterogeneous Data Sources – An ETANA-DL Case Study. Master's thesis, Virginia Tech CS Department, April 2004. `http://scholar.lib.vt.edu/theses/available/etd-04262004-153555/` [last visited July 4, 2012]. 24, 62

[88] U. Ravindranathan, R. Shen, M. A. Gonçalves, W. Fan, E. A. Fox, and F. Flanagan. Prototyping Digital Libraries Handling Heterogeneous Data Sources - the ETANA-DL Case Study. In *Proc. 8th European Conf. Research and Advanced Technology for Digital Libraries, ECDL*, number 3232 in LNCS, pages 186–197, Bath, UK, Sept. 2004. Springer-Verlag. DOI: 10.1007/978-3-540-30230-8_18 62

[89] U. Ravindranathan, R. Shen, M. A. Gonçalves, W. Fan, E. A. Fox, and J. W. Flanagan. ETANA-DL: managing complex information applications – an archaeology digital library. In *JCDL '04: Proceedings of the 4th ACM/IEEE-CS Joint Conference on Digital Libraries*, pages 414–414, New York, NY, USA, 2004. ACM Press. DOI: 10.1145/996350.996481 24, 62

[90] RDF. Resource Description Framework, http://www.w3.org/rdf/. 55

[91] T. C. Redman. *Data Quality – Management and Technology*. Bantam Books, New York, 1992. 16

[92] J. Rothenberg. *Using Emulation to Preserve Digital Documents*. Koninklijke Bibliotheek, The Netherlands, 2000. 10

[93] M. Rowan, P. Gregor, D. Sloan, and P. Booth. Evaluating web resources for disability access. In *Fourth Annual ACM Conference on Assistive Technologies*, pages 80–84, Arlington, Virginia, 2000. ACM. DOI: 10.1145/354324.354346 5

[94] N. Ryan. Managing complexity: Archaeological information systems past, present and future. In *Proc. British Association Annual Festival of Science, University of Birmingham, 8-13 Sept.*, 1996. 60

[95] S. Sanett. The Cost to Preserve Authentic Electronic Records in Perpetuity: Comparing Costs across Cost Models and Cost Frameworks. *RLG DigiNews*, 7(4), August 2003. http://www. rlg.org/preserv/diginews/v7_n4_feature2.html. 11

[96] T. Saracevic. Relevance: a review and a framework for thinking on the notion in information science. *Journal of the American Society for Information Science*, 26:321–343, 1975. DOI: 10.1002/asi.4630260604 13

[97] T. Saracevic. Relevance reconsidered. In *Information science: Integration in perspectives.Proceedings of the Second Conference on Conceptions of Library and Information Science.Copenhagen (Denmark)*, pages 201–218, 1996. DOI: 10.1002/(SICI)1097-4571(199404)45:3%3C124::AID-ASI2%3E3.0.CO;2-8 13

[98] T. Saracevic. Digital library evaluation: Toward evolution of concepts. *Library Trends*, 49(2):350–369, 2000. 2

[99] T. Saracevic. Evaluation of digital libraries: an overview. Technical report, Rutgers University, 2004. 2, 3, 4

[100] T. Saracevic and L. Covi. Challenges for digital library evaluation. In *Proceedings of the 63rd Annual Meeting of the American Society for Information Science*, volume 37, pages 341–350, 2000. 2

[101] K. Sayood. *Introduction to Data Compression*. Morgan Kaufmann Publishers, 2929 Campus Drive, Suite 260, San Mateo, CA 94403, USA, 1996. 12

[102] J. Schloen. Archaeological Data Models and Web Publication Using XML. *Computers and the Humanities*, 35(2):123–152, 2001. DOI: 10.1023/A:1002471112790 61

[103] R. Shen. *Applying the 5S Framework to Integrating Digital Libraries*. Ph.D. dissertation, Virginia Tech CS Department, Blacksburg, Virginia, 2006. `http://scholar.lib.vt.edu/theses/available/etd-04212006-135018/` [last visited July 4, 2012]. xv, xvi, xxi, 2, 50, 52, 54, 62, 63, 65, 66, 67, 68, 69

[104] R. Shen, M. A. Gonçalves, W. Fan, and E. A. Fox. Requirements Gathering and Modeling of Domain-Specific Digital Libraries with the 5S Framework: An Archaeological Case Study with ETANA. In *Proc. European Conference on Digital Libraries, ECDL 2005, Vienna, Sept. 18-23*, pages 1–12. Springer, 2005. `http://dl.acm.org/citation.cfm?id=2142714` [last visited July 4, 2012]. xvi, 24, 62, 63, 65, 66, 67, 68, 69

[105] R. Shen, N. S. Vemuri, W. Fan, and E. A. Fox. What is a successful digital library? In *ECDL'06*, pages 208–219, 2006. DOI: 10.1007/11863878_18 3

[106] R. Shen, N. S. Vemuri, W. Fan, and E. A. Fox. Integration of complex archeology digital libraries: An ETANA-DL experience. *Information Systems*, 33(7-8):699–723, 2008. `http://dx.doi.org/10.1016/j.is.2008.02.006` [last visited July 4, 2012]. DOI: 10.1016/j.is.2008.02.006 xvi, 24, 62, 63, 65, 66, 67, 68, 69

[107] H. G. Small. Co-citation in the scientific literature: A new measure of the relationship between two documents. *Journal of the American Society for Information Science*, 24(4):265–269, July-Aug. 1973. DOI: 10.1002/asi.4630240406 15, 42

[108] H. Suleman. *Open Digital Libraries*. Ph.D. thesis, Virginia Tech CS Department, Blacksburg, Virginia, 2002. `http://scholar.lib.vt.edu/theses/available/etd-11222002-155624/` [last visited July 4, 2012]. 24, 26, 58

[109] H. Suleman. Interoperability in digital libraries. In T.-E. Synodinou and S. Kapidakis, editors, *DE-Publishing and Digital Libraries: Legal and Organizational Issues*, chapter 2, pages 31–47. IGI Global, Iglezakis, Ioannis, 2010. 50

[110] H. Suleman and E. Fox. Leveraging OAI harvesting to disseminate theses. *Library Hi Tech*, 21(2):219–227, 2003. DOI: 10.1108/07378830310479857 57

[111] H. Suleman and E. A. Fox. Beyond harvesting: Digital library components as OAI extensions. Technical report, Virginia Tech, 2002. 57

[112] H. Suleman, E. A. Fox, and M. Abrams. Building quality into a digital library. In *Proceedings of the Fifth ACM Conference on Digital Libraries: DL '00, June 2-7, 2000, San Antonio, TX.* ACM Press, New York, 2000. June 4-7, 2000. DOI: 10.1145/336597.336669 26

[113] R. S. Taylor. Question-negotiation and information seeking in libraries. *College and Research Libraries*, 29:178–194, 1968. 9

[114] S. Tönnies and W. tilo Balke. Using semantic technologies in digital libraries: a roadmap to quality evaluation. In *ECDL 2009*, pages 168–179, 2009. DOI: 10.1007/978-3-642-04346-8_18 2

[115] B. ten Cate, V. Dalmau, and P. Kolaitis. Learning schema mappings. In *ICDT 2012*, pages 182–195, 2012. DOI: 10.1145/2274576.2274596 58

[116] G. Tsakonas, S. Kapidakis, and C. Papatheodorou. Evaluation of user interaction in digital libraries. *DELOS Workshop on the Evaluation of Digital Libraries*, 2004. 2

[117] G. Tsakonas and C. Papatheodorou. An ontological representation of the digital library evaluation domain. *JASIST*, 62(8):1577–1593, 2011. DOI: 10.1002/asi.21559 2

[118] S. Virkus, G. A. Alemu, T. A. Demissie, B. J. Kokollari, M. E. L. M., and D. Yadav. Integration of digital libraries and virtual learning environments: a literature review. In *New Library World*, volume 110 (3/4), pages 136–150, 2009. DOI: 10.1108/03074800910941338 49

[119] E. M. Voorhees. Evaluation by highly relevant documents. In *Proceedings of the 24th Annual International ACM SIGIR Conference on Research and Development in Information Retrieval*, pages 74–82, 2001. DOI: 10.1145/383952.383963 9

[120] Y. Wand and R. Y. Wang. Anchoring data quality dimensions in ontological foundations. *Communications of the ACM*, 39(11):86–95, Nov. 1996. DOI: 10.1145/240455.240479 22

[121] A. Waugh, R. Wilkinson, B. Hills, and J. Dell'oro. Preserving digital information forever. In *DL'00: Proceedings of the 5th ACM International Conference on Digital Libraries*, pages 175–184, San Antonio, Texas, 2000. DOI: 10.1145/336597.336659 10

[122] B. Zhang, M. A. Gonçalves, and E. A. Fox. An OAI-Based Filtering Service for CITIDEL from NDLTD. In *Proc. of the 6th International Conference on Asian Digital Libraries, ICADL 2003*, pages 590–601, Kuala Lumpur, Malaysia, December 8-12, 2003. DOI: 10.1007/b94517 17

[123] Y. Zhang. Developing a holistic model for digital library evaluation. *J. Am. Soc. Inf. Sci. Technol.*, 61(1):88–110, Jan. 2010. DOI: 10.1002/asi.21220 3

[124] Q. Zhu. 5SGraph: A Modeling Tool for Digital Libraries. Masters thesis, Virginia Tech Dept. of Computer Science, 2002. http://scholar.lib.vt.edu/theses/available/etd-11272002-210531/ [last visited July 4, 2012]. 62

[125] Q. Zhu, M. A. Gonçalves, R. Shen, L. Cassel, and E. A. Fox. Visual semantic modeling of digital libraries. In *Proc. 7th European Conference on Digital Libraries (ECDL 2003), 17-22 August, Trondheim, Norway, Springer LNCS 2769*, pages 325–337. Springer, 2004. 62

Authors' Biographies

EDWARD A. FOX

Edward A. Fox grew up on Long Island, New York. He attended the Massachusetts Institute of Technology (MIT), receiving a B.S. in 1972 in Electrical Engineering, through the Computer Science option. His undergraduate adviser was J.C.R. Licklider. His thesis adviser was Michael Kessler. At MIT he founded the ACM Student Chapter and the Student Information Processing Board, receiving the William Stewart Award.

From 1971–1972 he worked as Data Processing Instructor at the Florence Darlington Technical College. From 1972–1978 he was Data Processing Manager at Vulcraft, a Division of NUCOR Corporation, also in Florence, SC. In the fall of 1978 he began his graduate studies at Cornell University in Ithaca, NY. His adviser was Gerard Salton. He received an M.S. in Computer Science in 1981 and a Ph.D. in 1983. From the summer of 1982 through the spring of 1983 he served as Manager of Information Systems at the International Institute of Tropical Agriculture, Ibadan, Nigeria. From the fall of 1983 through the present he has been on the faculty of the Department of Computer Science at Virginia Tech (also called VPI&SU or Virginia Polytechnic Institute and State University). In 1988 he was given tenure and promoted to the rank of Associate Professor. In 1995 he was promoted to Professor.

Dr. Fox has been a member of ACM since 1968. He was Vice Chairman of ACM SIGIR 1987–1991. Then he was Chair 1991–1995. During that period, he helped launch the new ACM SIG on Multimedia. He served as a member of the ACM Publications Board 1988-1992 and as

Editor-in-chief of ACM Press Database and Electronic Products 1988–1991, during which time he helped conceive and launch the ACM Digital Library. He served 2000–2006 as a founder and Co-editor-in-chief of the ACM Journal of Education Resources In Computing (JERIC), which led to the ACM Transactions on Education. Over the period 2004–2008 he served as Chairman of the IEEE-CS Technical Committee on Digital Libraries, and continues to serve on its Executive Committee. Dr. Fox served 1995–2008 as Editor of the Morgan Kaufmann Publishers, Inc. Series on Multimedia Information and Systems. He has been a member of Sigma Xi since the 1970s and a member of Upsilon Pi Epsilon since 1998.

In 1987 Dr. Fox began to explore the idea of all students shifting to electronic theses and dissertations (ETDs), and has worked in this area ever since. He led the establishment of the Networked Digital Library of Theses and Dissertations (operating informally starting in 1995, incorporated in May 2003). He serves as founder and Executive Director of NDLTD. He won its 1st Annual NDLTD Leadership Award in May 2004.

Dr. Fox has been involved in a wide variety of professional service activities. He has chaired scores of conferences and workshops, and served on hundreds of program and conference committees. At present he serves on more than ten editorial boards, and is a member of the board of directors of the Computing Research Association (CRA; he is co-chair of its membership committee, as well as a member of CRA-E, its education committee). He also chairs the steering committee of the ACM/IEEE-CS Joint Conference on Digital Libraries.

Dr. Fox has been (co)PI on over 113 research and development projects. In addition to his courses at Virginia Tech, Dr. Fox has taught over 78 tutorials in more than 28 countries. His publications and presentations include: 16 books, 106 journal/magazine articles, 49 book chapters, 180 refereed (+40 other) conference/workshop papers, 58 posters, 66 keynote/banquet/international invited/distinguished speaker presentations, 38 demonstrations, and over 300 additional presentations. His research and teaching has been on digital libraries, information storage and retrieval, hypertext/hypermedia/multimedia, computing education, computational linguistics, and sub-areas of artificial intelligence.

MARCOS ANDRÉ GONÇALVES

Marcos André Gonçalves is an Associate Professor at the Computer Science Department of the Universidade Federal de Minas Gerais (UFMG), Brazil. He holds a Ph.D. in Computer Science (CS) from Virginia Tech (2004), a M.S. in CS from State University of Campinas, Brazil (Unicamp, 1997), and a B.S., also in Computer Science, from the Federal University of Ceará, Brazil (UFC, 1995). Professor Gonçalves has served as referee on different journals (TOIS, TKDE, IP&M, Information Retrieval, Information Systems, etc.) and at several conferences (SIGIR, CIKM, JCDL, TPDL, etc.). His research interests include information retrieval, digital libraries, text classification and text mining in general, having published more than 150 refereed journal articles and conference papers in these areas. Marcos is currently an affiliate member of the Brazilian Academy of Sciences.

RAO SHEN

Rao Shen received her Ph.D. in Computer Science from Virginia Tech in 2006. Her advisor was Edward A. Fox. Her research interests include digital libraries, information retrieval, information visualization, and machine learning. She joined the Web search relevance team at Yahoo! in May 2006. She is working on problems related to federated search in Yahoo! Labs.

Printed in the United States
by Baker & Taylor Publisher Services